Marion and Theology

D1570488

PHILOSOPHY AND THEOLOGY SERIES

Other titles in the Philosophy and Theology series include:

Marion and
Theology

Christina M. Gschwandtner

Bloomsbury T&T Clark
An imprint of Bloomsbury Publishing Plc

B L O O M S B U R Y
LONDON • OXFORD • NEW YORK • NEW DELHI • SYDNEY

Bloomsbury T&T Clark

An imprint of Bloomsbury Publishing Plc

Imprint previously known as T&T Clark

50 Bedford Square	1385 Broadway
London	New York
WC1B 3DP	NY 10018
UK	USA

www.bloomsbury.com

BLOOMSBURY, T&T CLARK and the Diana logo are trademarks of Bloomsbury Publishing Plc

First published 2016

© Christina M. Gschwandtner, 2016

Christina M. Gschwandtner has asserted her right under the Copyright, Designs and Patents Act, 1988, to be identified as Author of this work.

British Library Cataloguing-in-Publication Data
A catalogue record for this book is available from the British Library.

ISBN: HB: 978-0-56766-022-0
PB: 978-0-56766-021-3
ePDF: 978-0-56766-023-7
ePub: 978-0-56766-024-4

Library of Congress Cataloging-in-Publication Data
Names: Gschwandtner, Christina M., 1974- author. Title: Marion and theology / Christina M. Gschwandtner. Description: New York : Bloomsbury T&T Clark, 2016. | Includes bibliographical references and index. Identifiers: LCCN 2015040642 | ISBN 9780567660220 Subjects: LCSH: Marion, Jean-Luc, 1946- | Spirituality–Christianity. | Theology. Classification: LCC B2430.M284 G727 2016 | DDC 210.92–dc23 LC record available at http://lccn.loc.gov/2015040642

Typeset by Fakenham Prepress Solutions, Fakenham, Norfolk NR21 8NN
Printed and bound in India

For
Laurie and Brenda Braaten
K. Steve McCormick

and in memory of
Gordon J. Thomas

CONTENTS

ABBREVIATIONS

The following abbreviations are employed for citations from works by Jean-Luc Marion:

BG   *Being Given: Toward a Phenomenology of Givenness* (trans. Jeffrey L. Kosky; Stanford, CA: Stanford University Press, 2002).

CpV   *Le croire pour le voir* (Paris: Parole et Silence, 2010; forthcoming in translation with Fordham University Press, 2016).

CQ   *Cartesian Questions: Method and Metaphysics* (Chicago: University of Chicago Press, 1999).

CV   *The Crossing of Visible* (trans. James K. A. Smith; Stanford, CA: Stanford University Press, 2004).

EG   *On the Ego and on God: Further Cartesian Questions* (trans. Christina M. Gschwandtner; New York: Fordham University Press, 2007).

EP   *The Erotic Phenomenon* (trans. Stephen E. Lewis; Chicago: University of Chicago Press, 2003).

GR   *Givenness and Revelation* (trans. Stephen E. Lewis; Oxford: Oxford University Press, 2016).

GWB   *God without Being* (trans. Thomas A. Carlson; Chicago: University of Chicago Press, 1991).

ID   *The Idol and Distance: Five Studies* (trans. Thomas A. Carlson; New York: Fordham University Press, 2001).

IE   *In Excess: Studies of Saturated Phenomena* (trans. Robyn Horner and Vincent Berraud; New York: Fordham University Press, 2002).

MP *On Descartes' Metaphysical Prism: The Constitution and the Limits of Onto-theo-logy in Cartesian Thought* (trans. Jeffrey A. Kosky; Chicago: University of Chicago Press, 1999).

NC *Negative Certainties* (trans. Stephen E. Lewis; Chicago: University of Chicago Press, 2015).

PC *Prolegomena to Charity* (trans. Stephen E. Lewis; New York: Fordham University Press, 2002).

RC *La rigueur des choses: Entretiens avec Dan Arbib* (Paris: Flammarion, 2012; forthcoming in translation with Fordham University Press, 2016).

RG *Reduction and Givenness: Investigations of Husserl, Heidegger, and Phenomenology* (trans. Thomas A. Carlson; Evanston: Northwestern University Press, 1998).

SP *In the Self's Place: The Approach of Saint Augustine* (trans. Jeffrey L. Kosky; Stanford, CA: Stanford University Press, 2012).

VR *The Visible and the Revealed* (New York: Fordham University Press, 2008).

Introduction

Jean-Luc Marion is one of the most important living French philosophers. Unlike in the case of most of the thinkers presented in this series, however, Marion's connections to theology permeate all of his philosophical writings. He is in fact often regarded as a theologian and his work alternately praised or chided for being deeply theological, although his French academic appointments have all been in philosophy and he consistently refuses the title of theologian and insists that his work is solely philosophical (on occasion even claiming that theology would be 'far too difficult'.) Yet certainly many of his books treat theological topics, self-identify as essays in theology (especially his best-known text in the English-speaking world, *God without Being*) or have theological implications. One might even say that a major impetus of Marion's more strictly philosophical work is precisely to open a space for serious thinking about the divine and other theological topics within philosophy. Much ink has been spilled on exactly where the boundary line between philosophy and theology lies – in Marion's own work or more generally – and how to police this border. This introduction to Marion's work will not attempt to resolve that particular question, which depends far too much not only on one's conception of philosophy but also on one's understanding of theology, but rather will present Marion's work *as* a theology or even as a kind of spirituality. This is obviously not to claim that this is the *only* or even necessarily the best way to read his project, but rather that it constitutes a particularly profitable or enriching way of reading him that sheds light both on Marion's work and on the activity of theology. 'Theology' is then here employed, at least initially, quite loosely – not referring to any particular approach to systematic theology, of which there are myriad – and what 'theology' means will emerge as much through the reading of Marion's work rather than being imposed on it in a priori fashion. (This is not to say, of course, that it emanates from some neutral or objective starting point without presuppositions, but rather that it proceeds from the hermeneutic principles of wagering that a text's meaning best emerges when it is read on its own terms and the interpreter seeks to enter it as deeply as possible, while always cycling hermeneutically between the text and the contemporary horizon.)

Jean-Luc Marion was born in 1946 as the son of a French and literature teacher and a weapons engineer in the French defence department. His father came from a family of engineers and had been imprisoned for resistance to the occupying Nazi forces from 1940 to 1945. A voracious reader of literature as a teenager, Jean-Luc took the unusual path of preparing for the prestigious École normale supérieure and the strenuous agrégation examination, passed by only a small fraction of those who attempt it, instead of following his uncles into the family factories. While still a student at the Condorcet preparatory school in Paris, a friend took him to Montmartre where he met Monsignor Maxime Charles and began the sustained practice of silent prayer before the blessed sacrament, which was to have a determinative and abiding influence on his theological and spiritual life. While pursuing his studies at the École (and, at the insistence of a couple of friends, having switched from literature to philosophy), he became involved in publishing the lay theological journal *Résurrection* and then a couple of years later became one of the founding members of the Francophone version of *Communio*, with which he and his wife Corinne have been intimately involved for decades. Having successfully passed the agrégation, he became assistant at the Sorbonne to the famous Descartes scholar Ferdinand Alquié, who had directed his master's thesis. In the seven years at the Sorbonne (1974–81) he successfully defended his doctoral theses on Descartes (the French system requires two different doctorates in order to qualify for a full university post and to be able to supervise research: the *doctorat de troisième cycle*, equivalent to a PhD and now called simply a *doctorat*; and the *doctorat d'état*, which permits the supervision of research, now called the *Habitilation à Diriger des recherches* or HDR for short) and published them, together with an index or concordance to Descartes' works. His first full university appointment was at Poitiers, where he also participated in extensive collaboration with Italian, Dutch, German and American Descartes scholars and first commenced travelling internationally. This is also where he started reading and teaching phenomenology more seriously. After seven years in Poitiers (1981–88), he moved to Nanterre, a progressive university in the Paris suburbs, where he taught for another seven years, while also chairing the department and various important committees.

In 1995 he was appointed to the chair of metaphysics at the Sorbonne, France's oldest and most prestigious university, where he taught until his retirement in 2012. Having begun regular appointments at the University of Chicago in the early 1990s, he was offered the John Nuveen chair previously held by Paul Ricœur in 2003 and in 2011 switched to the Andrew Greeley and Grace McNichols Greeley chair, after David Tracy's retirement from the Divinity School. In 2008 he was elected to assume the late Cardinal Jean-Marie Lustiger's chair at the Académie française, probably the highest honour French intellectual life has to bestow (the forty members of the Académie française, which was founded by Richelieu in 1635, are usually literary scholars or famous writers; they are considered the guardians of the French language and referred to as 'the immortals'). Retired from the Sorbonne, he continues teaching in Chicago and at the Institut catholique in Paris, and lectures all over the world. He and Corinne have two sons and several grandchildren.

Theologically, Marion was shaped deeply by his encounter with Maxime Charles, who sought to bring together theological training and vibrant parish life and inspired scores of students and young people. Marion learnt and taught in this ecclesial community at Montmartre, essentially getting a full theological education on the side. He also knew Cardinal Lustiger early on, long before he became cardinal, and assisted him extensively when Lustiger became archbishop of Paris, writing lectures and addresses for him or helping him with research. He was recruited together with several other young scholars to assist Jean Daniélou in starting the Francophone version of the Roman Catholic lay theological journal *Communio* and, after Daniélou's untimely death, the group suddenly found itself in charge of launching and publishing the journal on Hans Urs von Balthasar's insistence; Marion was its editor-in-chief (together with Rémi Brague) for the first ten years. Marion knew closely several of the luminaries of the ressourcement movement in France, some of the most significant Catholic theologians of the twentieth century – many of whom also deeply shaped the Second Vatican Council: Henri de Lubac, Jean Daniélou and especially Louis Bouyer. Their recovery of Patristic theology, push for liturgical renewal and vibrant spirituality, and scholarship on and devotion to the sacramental life shaped Marion profoundly, as did the friendship and mentoring he received from Maxime Charles, Hans Urs von Balthasar and Jean-Marie Lustiger.

Marion stems from a deeply Catholic family that was aligned with reform and resistance, fiercely loyal to de Gaulle. Although he was quite active in the Catholic student movement early on, he became disenchanted with its strident activism and at times is fairly critical of attempts to make Catholicism 'relevant' or 'engaged'. He is also insistent that he is not a 'Catholic philosopher' and claims, like Heidegger, that this term makes no more sense than 'Protestant physics' or 'Catholic shoemaking'. Rather he thinks of himself as a philosopher whose philosophy should be judged solely on its merits of being philosophical, a philosopher who also happens to be – or is trying to become – Catholic (RC, 284–5).

In this book I will provide not only an introduction to Marion's extensive work but also show that his project can be read as advocating a lived theology – a spirituality that is also a theology, a theology that is grounded in prayer and spiritual practice. Marion speaks of the impact the adoration of the sacrament had and continues to have on him:

> The discovery of the prayer of eucharistic adoration was a fundamental thing. Maxim Charles insisted on this point: It is a form of objective prayer, of objective mysticism. Its goal is to achieve or develop (in the photographic, psychological, and almost phenomenological sense) the link between, on the one side, biblical texts that convey God's words or often Christ's words, and, on the other side, a totally real, but perfectly silent, presence. The whole work of contemplation consists in making these two coincide or at least to bring them closer together. It consists in putting into focus what will make presence speak, what will give

to the words their referent. It is a labour of attention, of concentration, but one that is essentially de-subjectivizing, where the *I* is erased before the one whom it observes speaking. That was a real and great discovery for me. The spiritual life, especially in the catholic religion, seems to privilege interiority in opposition to the exteriority of action (apostolic or secular); but one must make it more than a subjective counterpart of what is real and is found in the world, with all attendant ambiguities. Yet, with eucharistic adoration, a fundamental psychological change takes place, since it is a matter of putting words into the mouth of a reality, if I can put it like this, or of causing the words spoken to be really those said by Someone who is here now, before me, infinitely more than me. (RC, 52–3)

Hence Marion interprets his experience of prayer as at the same time a guidance toward rigorous thinking about God. The experience of God's presence and reality in the spiritual discipline of prayer and adoration opens the possibility for unfolding and explicating what is manifested there. He suggests that the consequence of this insight is that 'one can no longer place speculative theology or neutral rationality to one side and the spiritual life to the other, but the same place encompasses both' (RC, 53). This is what this book will develop more fully: a theology that is also a spirituality, a spirituality that is also deeply theological. And I contend that this impetus is visible throughout Marion's work, from his early writings on Descartes to his most recent, such as the 2014 Gifford Lectures. Marion's description of prayer before the blessed sacrament applies not only to eucharistic adoration but to his project as a whole: to his description of the self, of love, of the saturated phenomenon and of the divine. This is what the rest of this book will establish by simultaneously introducing the major components of Marion's work to the reader.

* * *

This book is dedicated to the teachers who shaped me most deeply theologically in college and immediately afterward. Laurie Braaten taught me how to read the Bible incarnationally and not be threatened by the methods of scriptural criticism, but also continually brought together the theoretical and the practical in his teaching of the

Hebrew Scriptures. He and his wife Brenda fed my body and spirit for years: with countless Sunday dinners and Sunday afternoon hikes in New England, northern Illinois and southern Wisconsin. What little I know about North American flora and fauna – and what little I've seen of it up close – I owe to them. They taught me to read both of God's books, Scripture and nature, to see how all of creation praises God and how God cares deeply about the land and its many creatures, whether in Exodus, in the psalms, in Hosea and Micah, on Mount Lafayette, Mount Chocorua, the Illinois prairie or at Devil's Lake State Park outside Madison, Wisconsin. I am deeply grateful for your immense generosity and abiding friendship.

Steve McCormick taught me that theology could be not only intellectually stimulating, but profoundly life-giving. Never will I forget discovering Irenaeus, Athanasius and the Cappadocians in his classes, learning about theosis and recapitulation, or discussing the absolute centrality of trinitarian and sacramental faith for the life of the church. My apologies for all the times my questions and objections must have driven you absolutely insane and thank you for making the life and thinking of the early church, the Nicene creed and the councils come alive for me. Thank you for challenging me, supporting me and for teaching me a theology characterized by a beauty, wonder and rigour that did not require me to hand in my brain.

Gordon Thomas was my mentor for my theology master's thesis on original sin and a mentor in many other ways as well. I have never before or since met anyone with such passion for living a holy life, such deep love for his church and such charisma for teaching and mentoring. Your teaching, life, passion and sincerity inspired and touched me profoundly. You are still deeply missed.

More recently I have also learned much theologically from Father Andrew Louth, supervisor of my theology PhD thesis at the University of Durham, Father John Behr, Dean of St Vladimir's Orthodox Theological Seminary, and Father Robert Arida, Dean and Rector of Holy Trinity Orthodox Cathedral in Boston, MA. I am grateful to them, as well as to Tracy Gustilo, Lisa Radakovich Holsberg and Gregory Tucker, who are always willing to discuss theology over a cup of tea and tolerate me in lots of other ways as well. Your friendship means more to me than I can possibly say.

My reading of Marion has obviously been shaped and responds to that of other scholars of his work, such as Kevin Hart, Stephen

Lewis, Tamsin Jones, Robyn Horner, Jeffrey Kosky, Thomas Carlson, Shane Mackinlay and many others. Their rich work, as well as conversations with younger scholars such as Bryne Lewis, Julia Reed, Stephanie Rumpza, Kadir Filiz, Nicolae Turcan, Donald Wallenfang, Stephen DeLay and others, at conferences and via email have continually enriched my own understanding of Marion's work. If I do not engage much of this secondary literature in this book explicitly, it is not because it is insignificant, but because this is meant to be an introduction to Marion's thought and so I have focused almost exclusively on the primary texts. My work has also profited from many fruitful discussions with students, in the last couple of years especially at Fordham University: many thanks to Bill Woody, Rob Duffy, Jesús Luzardo, Bruno Cassarà and Brock Mason in this respect. A special thanks to Stephen Lewis, not only for his excellent translations of Marion's work, but also for permitting me to work with his translation of the Gifford Lectures before their actual publication. I am grateful also for Anna Turton's and Miriam Cantwell's welcome of this book into the series at T&T Clark/Bloomsbury and for their help in steering this process to successful completion, and for Moira Eagling's careful copy-editing.

Special gratitude is obviously above all due in this case to Jean-Luc Marion who has been invariably gracious and generous in answering my many questions over the years and whose work inspired all of this in the first place. I hope he will not find his texts and arguments misrepresented too much in this introduction to his thought.

1

Addressing God

The question of appropriate language for the divine motivates much
of Marion's work and has done so for a long time – far longer than
most people realize who only read his phenomenological writings.
Not only is it central to one of his earliest more theologically
oriented books *Idol and Distance*, but it is already a main topic
in his first engagements with Descartes and the late medieval/early
modern context in which Descartes formulated his philosophy. In
this chapter I will prepare the ground for discussions of Marion's
writings in phenomenology by delineating the main contours of
his work on Descartes, showing both how they prepare for his
theological and phenomenological arguments and how they are
motivated by a similar theological and spiritual impetus to that
which characterizes his better-known works. Marion examines
appropriate language for the divine in various ways throughout
his work on Descartes and ultimately shows that talking *about*
God, as theology ostensibly does, cannot be separated from talking
to God. Speaking about God must lead to addressing God. I will
focus on four central themes: (1) onto-theo-logy and the causa sui;
(2) the creation of the eternal truths and the question of analogy;
(3) apophasis and the language of praise; and (4) the three ways
and proofs for God's existence. Several of these themes are closely
connected to each other.

1. Onto-theo-logy and the causa sui

Marion's first study of Descartes, initially a doctoral thesis, focuses on the question of ontology in Descartes. Marion undertakes to examine the metaphysical status of Descartes' work, inspired by Nietzsche's call to overcome or end metaphysics and Heidegger's delineation of the history of the demise of metaphysics and his call for its 'destruction' (or 'deconstruction'). The focus of Marion's investigation initially is a comparatively unexamined early text by Descartes, entitled *Rules for the Direction of the Mind*, which he suggests constituted Descartes' attempt to rewrite the curriculum for learning in the Jesuit schools in which he was educated. The teaching of Aristotle dominated the curriculum, so Marion's central thesis in *Descartes' Grey Ontology* (not yet translated into English) is that Descartes is engaging in an unacknowledged polemic with Aristotle, overturning his methods of reaching knowledge at every turn. Descartes does not employ the term 'metaphysics' for what he is doing and Marion asserts that Descartes' most famous work was deliberately called *Meditations on First Philosophy* and not 'Metaphysical Meditations', as the French translator named it. But does that mean that Descartes is not doing metaphysics? Quite the opposite. Marion suggests that in Descartes' work metaphysical claims are 'greyed' or dissimulated (hence the title 'grey ontology') through an epistemology, an account of knowledge. In order to demonstrate this, Marion employs Heidegger's definition of metaphysics in terms of onto-theo-logical constitution.

In his essay on 'The onto-theological constitution of metaphysics', originally a lecture on Leibniz and Hegel, Heidegger had argued that metaphysics is always characterized by an ontology and a theology that are mutually implicated in each other. That is to say, metaphysics is the kind of knowledge or science that speaks of all beings and their ways of being (thus provides an ontology), while simultaneously grounding these beings in one supreme or highest being, usually a divine being (thus a theology). These two are always wrapped up with each other: because the highest being is also a being, it belongs to ontology; but because all beings depend on the supreme being, they are all implicated in the theology. Furthermore, the supreme being, Heidegger asserts, usually takes the form of the causa sui, of a self-caused cause. This divine being is hence a philosophical formulation of 'God' and not the God of worship or devotion – Heidegger famously said that one could not dance or sing before this God or be inspired to awe or prayer. Finally, Heidegger argues that the question of Being as such and its difference from beings or even the 'beingness' of beings is actually forgotten in this construction. Metaphysics forgets 'ontological difference' and its grounding (of the supreme being on being and of beings on the supreme being) is inherently circular.

Marion takes this to be an excellent definition of the *structure* of metaphysics, i.e. of the form that metaphysics always takes, while maybe changing some of the particular content, depending on the specific version of the metaphysical system under examination. He confirms this by showing that Descartes' system can be read as precisely such a construct and hence that his philosophy can be considered a metaphysics even when he is not using the term or even explicitly focusing on ontological questions. But it emerges that Descartes' metaphysics is quite complicated, because in fact it is characterized by two (or possibly even three) such versions of metaphysics; Descartes deploys a *doubled* onto-theo-logy. This is manifested by a shift in Descartes' thinking during the *Meditations*. In Descartes' earlier work, especially the *Discourse on Method*, the supreme being is the *ego cogito*. The ego exists because it thinks and all other things exist because they are thought by the ego. Thus all being, everything that is, is dependent on the ego's thinking. The ego is the supreme being that grounds the being of all other beings. This is the metaphysics of the ego (or of the *cogitatio*, i.e. of the ego as thinking). In the *Meditations*, however, Descartes suspects that the ego might not be able to ground its own being all the time: What happens when the ego is not doubting or thinking? Can it sustain itself in being? So Descartes proceeds to formulate a second metaphysical construction. In this case, the supreme being is God, who is proven to exist in the Third Meditation, a being that the ego cannot ground and who hence becomes the one who holds even the ego in being and consequently also grounds all other beings. This is the metaphysics of the causa sui, of God as the cause of everything, including ultimately even himself (MP, 67–127).

Marion points out that Descartes is the first one to affirm the concept of the causa sui (EG, 139–60). While several medieval thinkers considered the causa sui, including Thomas Aquinas, they all rejected it as an incoherent notion: no one, not even God, could be his or her own cause. But Descartes affirms this idea for the case of God. It is later picked up by Spinoza, although most subsequent thinkers also reject it. Descartes' strong affirmation of the causa sui is hence fairly unique in the tradition. This alone proves the metaphysical character of Descartes' thinking, although, as we will see, there are also aspects of his thinking that will escape this strong metaphysical character. Marion suggests that the causa sui constitutes the culmination of the parallels between human and divine in Descartes' work. It cements God's autarchy and independence, modelled on the human autarchy of the will Descartes had established earlier. At the same time, it submits God to being and causality in Descartes' system (or, more exactly, in one of his systems) by making him the supreme arbiter of both.

In his most recent work on Descartes, which considers Descartes' writings on the soul and the passions, Marion actually suggests that in these very latest writings Descartes might have begun to formulate a third metaphysical construction, one that escapes the other two by formulating a moral ego. In the final meditation the ego emerges as passive, as 'feeling' or experiencing itself. The sensations of the flesh and the passions enable a different kind of knowing, one of feeling or sensing. This argument has not influenced Marion's thinking about God as fully – although it is itself influenced by his phenomenological analysis of the receptive self – so will not feature as prominently here.

The first effect of this explication of the onto-theo-logical constitution of metaphysics in Descartes consists in its deeply problematic claims about the divine. God becomes a philosophical and logical construct: a self-caused cause, a grounding of all being, an originator of causality and being who is ultimately himself (or maybe better, itself) dependent on causality and being. God becomes – in language we will more fully encounter in the next chapter – an idol. While Marion carefully explicates how Descartes' system is metaphysical, he also censures it: Here is a way how *not* to talk about God. To make God subject to metaphysics, to turn God into a being or cause, even the supreme being or a self-caused cause, is inappropriate. Blasphemous. We hence have a first clear, albeit 'negative', result: Metaphysics is not the way to talk about God. God is not just a being in a system, a cog in the metaphysical wheel – even if it is the central cog that makes the whole thing run.

Yet Marion's discussion of Descartes' metaphysics is profitable not just for understanding how Descartes' epistemology might be read as making ontological claims and how it might make God subject to metaphysics. Rather, Marion concludes that Descartes' rigorous metaphysical system, especially in its doubled construction, is *novel*, that he is the first one to inaugurate metaphysics in its modern formulation. And this means that onto-theo-logy is an essentially *modern* formulation, one that begins with Descartes and possibly ends with Heidegger, although we are certainly still grappling with its residues. This implies that the medieval thinkers might not have been metaphysical in this sense and might not have included God in metaphysics:

> Perhaps God does not enter truly into metaphysics before Descartes seizes him in it ... But, if this were the case, one would have to revise fundamentally the question of the metaphysical status of all medieval thought: being unaware not only of the principle of sufficient reason, but above all of its application to the essence of God, hence refusing unanimously the concept of the causa sui, the medieval thinkers could, at least partially, be removed from the onto-theological constitution of metaphysics and hence from an idolatrous interpretation of God. (EG, 160)

Marion shows this more fully for three of the most important thinkers: Anselm of Canterbury (especially his supposed 'proof' for God's existence), Augustine (especially the *Confessions*) and Aquinas. While Marion had initially suggested in *God without Being* that Aquinas might make God subject to metaphysics by speaking of him as the highest being, he makes clear in 'Aquinas and Onto-theo-logy' (an article now included in the revised 2012 edition of *God without Being*) that Aquinas does not fall into metaphysics and that he does not ultimately limit God to the question of being. (This essay is also maybe the clearest and fullest explication of the onto-theo-logical structure of metaphysics, as Marion understands it.)

There are thus two important results for theology of Marion's investigations into Cartesian metaphysics. On the one hand, metaphysics as onto-theo-logically constituted cannot speak appropriately of the divine because God is reduced to a function of grounding within a system. To speak of God appropriately, non-metaphysical language must be found. Any talk about God must preserve the divine transcendence and otherness. No talk that makes God subject to human parameters can ever do the job. On the other hand, theologians can draw on patristic and medieval thinkers for such insight, precisely because they were *not* metaphysical in their talk about God. And Heidegger's treatment has actually done us a tremendous service here, in Marion's view. Heidegger's definition of metaphysics has proven enormously helpful in outlining its parameters and understanding its structure. Applying it to medieval and modern authors helps to discern their respective contributions to metaphysics and aids in judging to what extent their discussions of the divine must be read with caution. The phenomenological analysis has become a useful filter for seeing past thinkers more clearly.

2. Eternal truths and analogy

While the investigation of Descartes' metaphysics confirms many of the assumptions we have about Descartes and shows him as the quintessentially modern thinker we usually take him to be, Marion also reveals another side to Descartes – a non-Cartesian side, if one might call it that. His second important study on Descartes, called the 'white theology', investigates claims Descartes made in three crucial letters he wrote in 1630 to Marin de Mersenne, a priest and scholar, who was friends not only with Descartes but also with Kepler and Galileo and various other early scientists. The question discussed in these letters concerns what are called the 'eternal truths': the truths of mathematics, logic and science, such as the principle of non-contradiction, the basic claims of geometry, and so forth. Many early scientists and philosophers had begun to argue that these principles are incontrovertible, that they are 'eternal' and immutable. God employs these principles for the creation of the world, not out of choice but out of necessity; they cannot be otherwise. If they were – if mathematical and geometrical truths were contingent on some decision of the divine and could be otherwise – they would be arbitrary and the creation of the world possibly a mere accident, which could well have had a different outcome or not have happened at all. Thus most thinkers at the time of Descartes had decided that these principles are necessary, eternal and uncreated. God uses them to create the world; no whim involved.

Descartes, as Marion shows, profoundly disagrees with this position. In one of his letters to Mersenne, Descartes argues that 'the mathematical truths that you call eternal have been laid down by God and depend on him entirely no less than the rest of his creatures'. This is the case, because 'to say that these truths are independent of God is to talk of him as if he were Jupiter or Saturn and to subject him to the Styx and the Fates'.[1] That is to say, to make God subject to the 'eternal truths' is blasphemous. That's no way to talk about God, the creator of all – even of mathematics, logic and geometry. Marion argues that the sentiment Descartes expresses in these letters about the eternal truths is absolutely determinative for Descartes' philosophy as a whole and informs it deeply. Marion's teacher at the Sorbonne, the famous Descartes scholar Ferdinand Alquié, had actually already suggested as much, but Marion carries this argument further by showing that Descartes is drawing on several medieval thinkers in articulating his position. For example, Descartes cites Suárez and Vasquez, something that had not been noticed before.

In his book on Descartes' white theology (not yet translated into English) Marion lays out this argument in great detail, showing how the entire late medieval and early modern period increasingly moves to univocal ways of talking about the divine. Descartes' thesis on the creation of the eternal truths resists this move. At the same time, Descartes refuses to become engaged in theology per se. His 'theology' is thus 'whitened out' or even 'blank' and 'innocent' (the French word *blanche* can have all of those connotations, just as *grise* in 'grey ontology' can mean not just 'grey' but also 'dissimulated' or 'obscured'). The tradition essentially recognizes three ways to talk about God. Either one uses equivocal language about the divine: God is radically different from everything created and next to nothing can be said of the divine and the human in common. Or one uses univocal language: God is very much like us and thus language that applies to the world or to humans can equally be used of God. In order to avoid these two extremes, both of which seem incorrect, the medieval period developed the notion of analogy: there is a similarity between God and us, although we are by no means identical. We can use human language to draw analogies between God and the world, while always recognizing that these analogies fall short and that they do not portray the divine adequately. Marion suggests that the doctrines of analogy had become increasingly obscured in the late Middle Ages (especially via Cajetan's mistaken interpretations and confused presentations of Aquinas' doctrine of analogy) and were no longer really available to Descartes. Yet, if analogy is no longer an option, then only univocity and equivocity remain. Most of the early modern period went the way of univocity and the eternal truths are one clear example of this: mathematics and logic apply equally to God and the world without distinction.

Yet, they are not the only example. Marion sets the discussion into a larger context of the demise of analogy and rise of univocity on several fronts: ontological, epistemological and spiritual. Thus thinkers like Suárez begin to use *ontological* language equally of God and the world: God is a being just like all other beings – maybe the supreme or the most powerful being, but still essentially a being. The same ontological language can be used of both creator and created, whether living beings or inanimate matter. All ultimately *is* or exists in similar fashion, even if God's existence is necessary while that of everyone and everything else is contingent, namely dependent upon God as supreme being. Kepler, Galileo and Mersenne take the *epistemological* path: God thinks and knows as we do, via mathematics, geometry and logic. The principles of knowledge are supreme and all thinking is subject to them, whether it is human thinking or God's. God's mind functions more or less exactly like ours, which is why we can know the logic of the creation and deduce knowledge about God from it. The univocity of knowing and the univocity of being ultimately combine, and both being and logic are seen to be prior and superior to God. Some mystical movements and thinkers, such as Bérulle, even asserted a kind of *spiritual* univocity between us and God, although they also stress God's incomprehensibility and transcendence. (Marion treats this third move far less and in other contexts speaks of it more positively; see EG, 167–9.) Descartes picks up on all these strains and holds them in ambivalent tension in his work.

Again, Marion shows a shift taking place in Descartes' thinking. In his early work, such as the *Rules for the Direction of the Mind* and some other early texts, Descartes speaks of a 'code' serving as foundation for 'simple natures'. These refer not to something inherent in the thing or being, but rather are the means of knowing the thing. In that sense they are part of Descartes' revolution of metaphysics into epistemology: what matters is not the essence of the thing but how it is known to the human mind. In fact, some of the simple natures are directly connected with the eternal truths, namely the mathematical parameters for making sense of the world. To understand the world is to crack this code, or as Kepler says, to 'think God's thoughts after him', to figure out the code God used to create the world. Descartes later abandons this language and terminology such as 'code', 'simple natures' and 'intuitus' (the human mind that imposes the code onto the world thus shaping it into a comprehensible object) disappears from his texts. Marion shows how the question of foundation, although it continues to be important to Descartes, is no longer linked to the question of creation. Throughout Descartes' work, knowledge becomes increasingly more grounded in the human mind, rather than in God's ordering of the world. Yet, Descartes argues most rigorously against his contemporaries' attempts to make the principles of the world entirely transparent and ultimately to make the divine creator superfluous (or at least entirely dependent on the logic of creation).

Here we encounter again a clear picture about appropriate and inappropriate ways of speaking of God, but in this case Descartes vacillates ambivalently between the right side and the wrong one. In his firm rejection of the idea that logic is superior to God, he shows us how not to speak of God, namely as a mere puppet of the principles of geometry. Descartes (and Marion) suggest that in Kepler and Galileo, God becomes like the ancient deities who were arbitrary and had very limited power. This is a blasphemous way of talking about the divine. Descartes thus helps us see how not to address God. He is not as successful a guide for finding a way beyond this. Due to the demise of the question of analogy, Descartes really has no way available to him to find a more appropriate way to talk about God. Marion presents him as finally taking recourse to the causa sui, precisely in order to get out of this dilemma about univocity, but this path is obviously a dangerous dead end, in Marion's view, because it ultimately subjects God to causality. Descartes' utter failure in this respect, despite his correct intuition that equivocal language is blasphemous and inappropriate, itself proves informative: 'among the things that are great

about Descartes, not the least was to have offered up his doubled
onto-theo-logy to the ordeal of these destitutions' (MP, 345).
Maybe any attempt to speak of the divine within the standard
parameters of knowing, especially as they are derived from science,
is doomed to failure.

Marion suggests that Pascal, contemporary of Descartes and
deeply influenced by his philosophy, attempts a more radical alternative: a different way of knowing altogether (the 'destitutions' in the
text just quoted refer to Pascal's challenge to Descartes). Two ideas
are important here – both for understanding this specific discussion
and for their larger influence on Marion's own work: the notion of
the 'three orders', and the evidence of the will or desire. Pascal formulates a famous distinction between three orders or ways of knowing.
Although it is grounded in an Augustinian distinction between three
types of concupiscence (lust of the flesh for pleasure, lust of the eyes
or the mind for curiosity, wilful pride for worldly ambition), Pascal
reformulates them more positively as different orders of knowing:
first that of the world, second that of the mind, and third that of
the heart. The first order of the world (or the 'flesh') is characterized by knowledge through the senses; it is mundane and general
knowledge, easily accessible to anyone. The second order, that of the
mind, is characterized by knowledge through thinking or rigorous
science and for Pascal is essentially identical with Descartes' system
of knowledge. Different rules apply here (namely the ones outlined
by Descartes in the *Rules* and other works) and this knowledge is
more difficult, not necessarily accessible to everyone. It is also quite
different from knowledge of the world and to move from the lower
to the higher order requires discipline, training and a transformation
of thinking, a different way of seeing. That is even truer for the move
to the third order, the order of the heart. Knowledge, or maybe rather
'wisdom', is gained here not through thinking but via affection and
love: this is also called the order of charity. When we love something
or someone, we come to know on an entirely different level that
has little to do with certainty. For Pascal, especially knowledge of
God is qualitatively different from philosophical ways of acquiring
knowledge. Love, then, is a kind of knowledge of the will that gives
access to a realm of phenomena that cannot be known otherwise.
The three levels or orders are incommensurable with each other and
while the higher can perceive the lower, the lower has no access to
the higher order. The higher level requires a kind of conversion that

is inconceivable from the lower level and cannot be understood on its terms (MP, 306–22).

Marion returns to this notion of the three orders over and over again in his work, often in theological contexts. He frequently identifies the third order of charity with theology. Theology refers to a knowledge of the heart that has its own kind of evidence, which is inaccessible from philosophy. Its phenomena remain foreign to the realm of knowledge, unless they are formulated in phenomenological terms and emptied to some extent of their own content. Thus, the ideas of charity or of linear notions of history, Marion suggests, are originally theological ideas that have been introduced into philosophical knowledge by being conceived philosophically and in some sense 'secularized' or 'generalized', hence becoming more widely accessible and open to philosophical investigation (VR, 74–9). At other times, Marion speaks of the third order more broadly as one in which love is the parameter of knowledge and hence a phenomenology of eros may also validly explore it. This 'saturated' phenomenality is of a higher order than the metaphysics of objects, which is an attempt to comprehend only applicable to objects that can be perceived clearly and distinctly in Descartes' sense. Pascal thus becomes the guide to a kind of knowledge that escapes Cartesian metaphysics, whether theologically or phenomenologically.

Pascal develops this idea of a knowledge of the heart also in some other places. He argues in several texts that for certain kinds of objects or phenomena, the evidence of clarity and distinctness, which Descartes advocates, is inappropriate and not an acceptable way of knowing because it obscures more than it reveals (EG, 63–79). The heart or even the desires of the will have their own evidence which functions in other ways that are not subject to logic and geometry. It is a method that convinces by 'pleasing' and not by logic. It provides its own kind of evidence, which appeals to and moves the will and the heart rather than the mind. Furthermore, this alternative type of 'knowledge' is particularly appropriate for matters of faith, where God is known 'hiddenly' or as unknowable. We thus only have a 'negative' knowledge of God, an obscure evidence of divine invisibility and incomprehensibility. Although Marion ultimately judges Pascal's elaboration of this method incomplete, he certainly thinks him to be going in the right direction. Phenomenology will supply the methodology that can develop Pascal's insights on this matter more fully. (At times Marion also likens this distinction between the two types of evidence – of the mind and of the will – to Immanuel Kant's distinction between theoretical and practical knowledge in the first and second critique, respectively.)

Again, a negative and a positive result have been achieved. On the one hand, univocal language for the divine is to be rejected. It is inappropriate, even blasphemous, to apply human logic and mathematical principles to God. A difference or distance between human and divine must always be maintained, although this is not an absolute difference, nor a complete equivocity that would allow no knowledge or talk about God at all. On the other hand, God might be approached with a very different kind of talk: one of desire, love and evidence susceptible to or even deriving from the will. This is indeed a kind of knowledge, but one whose methods and evidence are quite different from metaphysical or merely logical ones. This alternative knowledge of the heart remains to be fully developed, but its distinction from the knowledge of the mind is already clearly visible.

3. Apophasis and the language of praise

The discussion of analogy has already indicated that the question of what language might be appropriate to speak of the divine was not foreign to the medieval thinkers. Indeed, even many patristic thinkers confront this question. Maybe the most extensive and most famous elaboration of how God is named appropriately is that of Dionysius the Areopagite (now often called Pseudo-Dionysius) in his *Mystical Theology* and *Divine Names*. Marion discusses Dionysius repeatedly and is deeply influenced by a particular reading of the patristic thinker's work.[2] His reading of Dionysius informs his discussion of Descartes and appropriate language for God in important ways and will thus be discussed briefly in this section. We will return to Descartes (and his connection to Dionysius) in the final section of this chapter. Marion contends that Dionysius outlines three ways of speaking about God. First, one might employ 'affirmative' or so-called kataphatic language, namely by affirming things or attributes of the divine: God is good, God is all-powerful, God is love, and so forth. But one quickly realizes that this affirmative language falls short. While it seems right to say that God is good, 'good' does not mean there what it usually means to us: God is not good in the sense that *we* speak of goodness. God is not good exactly like us, because our version of 'goodness' falls far short of the divine. Similarly, God's power is not like human power: it is not grasping, arbitrary and vicious. Somehow it is not quite right to say that God is powerful. We are thus led to deny statements about the divine or to use 'negative' or 'apophatic' language: God is not evil, God is not grasping, but also God is not good in our sense of goodness, not powerful in our sense of power, and so forth. We must thus go beyond both ways of attempting to describe God, beyond both positive and negative language about the divine, to a very different kind of speech. Traditionally, this is a kind of 'hyper-eminent' way of speaking: God is super-good, beyond good; God is all-powerful, beyond any notions of human power, and so forth. Yet Marion insists that this is not just a third attempt at description, but actually a transformation of language. In this third way, language no longer predicates anything of the divine, no longer seeks to describe at all, but rather turns from description to praise or prayer. Instead of speaking *about* God, it speaks *to* God, it addresses God.

Although the most well-known articulation of this position is in a debate with Jacques Derrida on the question of the gift at the 1997 Villanova conference on the theme of 'God, the Gift, and Postmodernism', Marion had already articulated his appropriation of Dionysius in *Idol and Distance*, where he posits Dionysius' thought as a successful way of getting beyond the impasses of Heidegger's ontological difference, Lévinas' language of alterity and Derridian *différance*. All three, Marion suggests, are attempts to deal with difference or distance, but they ultimately all remain unsuccessful, as do those of Nietzsche and Hölderlin, who are the main figures discussed in Part I and Part II of the book, respectively (see the following chapter for a discussion of these earlier sections). The third part of *Idol and Distance* articulates this in terms of the terminology of withdrawal and advent by drawing on Dionysius' work extensively. Instead of serving as the referent of a discourse or the object of an investigation, God comes to us as unspeakable, unthinkable and incomprehensible (ID, 143). The very impossibility of defining or comprehending God becomes a kind of insight about the divine – or, maybe better, a confrontation or encounter with God. Instead of naming God, we receive a name: the name of Christ who comes in the name of God. The divine name is received as a gift of love (ID, 145). In this context, Marion focuses on Dionysius' terminology of *aitia*, usually translated as 'cause', which Marion here renders as 'requisite'. *Aitia* is linked not to knowledge or predication but to praise: God is praised or 'hymned' as the one outside or beyond all naming. Renouncing any attempt at comprehension (by predication) allows us to receive ourselves from divine goodness manifested in and across distance. If the distance were erased, genuine encounter and loving relation would be impossible. This is true both of inter-trinitarian relations and of divine-human encounter or participation. Distance is crossed, but not erased, in loving exposure to the divine. *Aitia*, then, refers to the prayer that asks or requests from the 'Requisite', the one who grants the prayer. Distance is traversed but not abolished (ID, 162).

Marion explores the Dionysian language of hierarchy as an indication for how to traverse distance, although he admits that this word has primarily negative connotations today. For Dionysius, in Marion's view, hierarchy refers to the sacred order of holiness and love, which gives itself freely, especially in Christ (ID, 162–80). And this gift is best received by being passed on ceaselessly (ID, 169). Again, praise is the most appropriate way to respond to this, the only way to maintain the distance that has been crossed in love. Marion here plays on the Greek term *logos*, used in the first chapter of the Gospel of John to speak of Christ as the word of God (ID, 180–95). Logos designates Christ, but also the peculiar rationality of discourse about the divine. Marion will return to this logos of Christianity, rooted in *the* Logos, Christ, in many of his contributions to *Communio* or more explicitly theological writings, always arguing that faith is not irrational, but supremely rational because rooted in the divine and incarnate logos. In *Idol and Distance* Marion contends that the divine logos delivers itself via the *logia* or words of God, hence enabling logia or speech about God as a kind of testimony to this kenotic gift. Language attempts to speak the unsayable not by articulating a referent or by appropriating categories, but by praising. This praise is not a veiled predication, but an articulation of a request, based on an 'as': I praise you 'as' x, not to state the truth of x, but to establish a relation between speaker and addressee. It performs the request within the prayer. Language has moved to address and action: prayer does not describe, but acts, and it does so with its own rigour. Heideggerian and maybe even Derridian speech remains metaphysical, while language about God must get outside of metaphysics and transgress it by opting for a different kind of address altogether.

Derrida takes this discussion up in a long footnote in an essay on negative theology, suggesting that even the so-called 'negative' or apophatic way is still predicating something of the divine, even as it denies certain descriptions and attributes. It is in response to this that at the first Villanova conference (later reprinted as the final chapter of *In Excess*; IE, 128–62) Marion formulates even more explicitly the third way as a performative, non-predicative way, a kind of talking that acts instead of depicting. It takes a position and elicits a response, rather than applying logic to God. He reiterates the threefold distinction between a kataphatic or affirmative, an apophatic or negative and a third way, which he here calls one of 'un-naming' – presumably in reference to Derrida's text on negative theology *Sauf le nom*, which means both 'without' the name and 'saving' the name, and the title of Derrida's essay 'How to Avoid Speaking: Denials'. The third way both says and undoes any saying of the divine name. Language thus acquires a pragmatic function. Praise does not attribute names to God, but answers to a call and moves the person at prayer closer to the divine. The third way, in Marion's view, escapes any onto-theo-logical structure and moves outside the horizon of being entirely. Instead of attributing 'being' or names to God, we receive our own 'being' and name in the baptismal prayer as we expose ourselves to the unknowable and incomprehensible and enter into the divine Name. Again, it is not a matter of comprehension, but a matter of encounter or relation, ultimately of 'the liturgical function of all *theo*-logical discourse' (IE, 157). Comprehension is transcended by exposure, holy terror before the divine alterity. In *The Erotic Phenomenon* (cf. EP, 144–50) and a couple of other essays (e.g. VR, 101–19) Marion returns to this threefold kind of language and applies it to the language of love, a language of the heart, that does not provide information but rather addresses the other, seeks to expose oneself to the other in expectation of a response. (We will return to this in Chapter 4 where I discuss Marion's analysis of love and the lover more fully.)

It may seem that we have left Descartes far behind, but indeed this discussion of 'negative' or 'mystical' theology is important for understanding Marion's work on Descartes – and its implications for theology – in a twofold manner. First, it is almost entirely parallel to the 'knowledge of the heart' or the 'order of charity' just outlined. The third way of talking about the divine is not just a little different, a little higher, a little superior to the other two, but it enters into a different kind of order, it is a transformation of speaking, rather than just a slight adjustment. It thus performs exactly the same kind of move that Marion has attempted to outline for Descartes and Pascal and with exactly the same intention: getting beyond restrictive, blasphemous speech about the divine and arriving instead at a language more appropriate for expressing God's transcendence and distance (and for bridging them) and ultimately for addressing God. Yet, there is a second, far closer, connection: Marion suggests that Descartes was familiar with this discussion about the divine names and has a stake in it. Descartes provides three proofs for God's existence in his work – all three can be found in the *Meditations* and the replies to objections that follow them – and the three proofs correspond to the three ways of naming God and are, in fact, an attempt to re-read or re-organize them. This attempt ultimately fails, but as with Descartes' other failures, the failure itself is instructive.

4. Proofs for God's existence

Descartes attempts to prove God's existence twice within the text of the *Meditations* itself. First, in the Third Meditation he shows that we have a clear and distinct idea of an infinite being and that we could not possibly have invented or constructed this idea. It is not a composite or mere extension of finite ideas. Finite and infinite are simply not on the same scale of extension: infinite does not just mean many finites put together or one finite after the other. Adding up does not get us to infinity. Hence there must be an infinite being that has actually endowed us with this idea we could not have invented. This naming of God as 'infinite' (*infinitum*) maintains firmly that God is incomprehensible and not subject to any human reasoning or methodology. Second, in the Fifth Meditation, Descartes switches instead to a proof from perfection that has some parallels to Anselm's so-called ontological proof (although Marion shows in a different article that Anselm's proof is not concerned with ontology but recognizes that the sort of knowledge we can have of God is always one that maintains the essential unknowability of the divine; cf. CQ, 139–60). God is a perfect and supreme being (*ens summe perfectum*). Thus, while the first is a negative claim about the divine (God is not finite, is utterly different from us, a thought we cannot invent) and is thus like the apophatic or negative way, the second is a positive or affirmative claim (God is perfect and all perfections can be attributed to him) and thus like the kataphatic way. In this second proof God is seen to function *within* the method and is hence quite comprehensible. Finally, in his reply to Caterus' objections in the 'Objections and Replies' published together with the *Meditations*, Descartes formulates the proof of the causa sui, a third 'definition' of the divine, which Marion here likens to the third way of eminence – at least in intention. Yet, in its identification of God with causality and power (*potentia*), it will ultimately come to function more like a form of predication and the naming of God as infinite will be shown to escape any sort of predication and hence to be more like the third way.

The three proofs for God's existence thus map onto various articulations of the three possible ways of naming the divine: Marion suggests that Descartes draws them not directly from Dionysius, but via medieval intermediaries such as Duns Scotus (for the first name of God as infinite), Ockham (for the definition of God as highest perfection), and somewhat more tentatively from Suárez for the causa sui. Yet, by drawing them from these more recent contexts, Descartes also reveals their incompatibility: Duns Scotus and Ockham, for example, were opposed to each other on precisely this issue (MP, 255–6). The three definitions cannot be employed simultaneously; they contradict each other. For example, while the second proof (in the Fifth Meditation) assigns a particular concept to God (namely that of perfection or omnipotence), the first proof in the Third Meditation, based on infinity, precisely speaks of the divine as an idea that escapes all concepts and transcends what we could imagine. Furthermore, the first and third ways also contradict each other. God cannot both be outside any notion of causality and function as supreme cause, even of his own being. Not all three ways can be pursued simultaneously. God cannot be both inside the method, as the

second proof and definition claims, and outside of it in incomprehensible fashion, as the first name of infinite maintains, both
outside causality and within it. In his attempt to move from one
to the other, Descartes clearly shows their incoherence and incompatibility. But this is again productive, as Marion points out in a
different context:

> The three conceptions of God Descartes offers in his metaphysics
> do not mesh with one another; indeed, they seem contradictory
> for the most part. This apparent inconsistency does not amount
> to a failure, however. Rather, it attests to the fact that God
> cannot adequately be conceived within the limited discourse
> of metaphysics. Descartes here boldly and explicitly confronts
> the tension between the demand for a conception of God that
> is intelligible to humans and respect for his transcendence. The
> fact that Descartes' metaphysical theology remains indeter-
> minate (white) and breaks down into several theses (just as
> light breaks down when it passes through a prism) makes it,
> somewhat paradoxically, *the* radical position on the question of
> God at the beginning of modern thought. (EG, 175)

In fact, here several things we have already discussed come
together: the three namings of God expressed by the three proofs
also correspond to the three metaphysical constructions. (a) The
name of God as perfection corresponds to the metaphysics of the
cogitatio which is a metaphysics of power (of knowing). It will be
taken up and developed further by Malebranche and other thinkers
who define God as 'infinitely perfect being' (EG, 179–81; see also
124–8). (b) The name of causa sui corresponds to the second
metaphysical construction concerned with causality. This definition
and articulation is worked out more fully in Leibniz and culminates
in his formulation of the 'principle of sufficient reason' and naming
of God as 'final reason' (EG, 180–1; see also 129–37). (c) The name
that escapes the two metaphysical systems, as Marion suggests in
On Descartes' Metaphysical Prism, or might correspond to the
more tentative Cartesian system developed in the final meditation
and his treatise on the *Passions of the Soul*, as Marion suggests
in *Sur la pensée passive de Descartes* (On Descartes' Passive
Thought), is the name of infinity. The notion of the 'infinite'
escapes the restrictive and blasphemous metaphysical namings that

attempt to make God subject to ontology, epistemology or any other human construct.

There is a sense in which Pascal both picks up on and rejects the Cartesian name of infinite – in an early fragment even calling it 'useless and uncertain' (MP, 289–306). And he condemns it precisely as blasphemous, as still maintaining too much continuity between human and divine, as still too philosophical. Pascal draws a radical distinction between 'the god of the philosophers' and the God of faith, 'the God of Abraham, Isaac and Jacob', claiming that the two have nothing to do with each other. Pascal radically rejects all attempts at proving God's existence, because, as Marion puts it, 'with God, it is less an issue of his existence than of our decision concerning him' (MP, 298). For Pascal, God is a God of love and relation, a hidden God we must encounter in Christ, not a philosophical conundrum. Thus Pascal draws strict distinctions between 'evidence', such as that deployed by Cartesian metaphysics, and 'charity', which does not operate according to any standard parameters of knowledge. Not only does Pascal's challenge to Descartes leave metaphysics 'destitute', that is, sets it aside as invalid and inoperative as regards the divine, but Pascal issues a fundamental warning to theological discourse: adopting a philosophical system is not only dangerous, but may well miss the reality of God and faith entirely. Speculation about God's nature or existence is futile; encountering God in love, prayer and a holy life is instead what matters. While Marion does not simply adopt Pascal's claims uncritically, his frequent recourse to the distinction between the three orders and his overall fairly positive treatment of Pascal indicates at the very least where his own preferences lie. He insists that this is not a rejection of knowledge per se or a descent into pure irrationality, but rather a plea for a different kind of knowledge, an alternative type of reason. We will encounter this claim repeatedly in various forms throughout Marion's work.

We reach thus again the same twofold insight in regard to language about God. Negatively speaking, any language that is metaphysical, that makes God subject to being or knowing or thinking, is inappropriate and must be firmly rejected. An alternative language must be found. We cannot and should not speak of God as the highest or supreme being and thus as one being among others, sharing a common way of being with them, even if in a superior mode. As Marion asks in his preface to the English translation of *God without Being*: 'With respect to Being, does God have to behave like Hamlet?' (GWB, xx). The implied answer clearly is 'no'. Similarly, God as supreme cause recreates the same problem in regard to causality, which is hence also inappropriate for the divine, especially in its iteration of the causa sui. We cannot and should not speak of God with the logic of mathematics or geometry; God does not know as we do, is not subject to concerns about necessity or contingency. Applying concepts to God or seeing God as the ground of all concepts are both ways of inscribing the divine within something that becomes ultimately superior, whether that is human rationality, mathematics, geometry, logic, causality or the principle of sufficient reason. This implies that theology should be very careful when adopting philosophical systems or parameters for its own exercise. Should theology seek to be a 'science'? What use should theology make of philosophical ways of thinking or specific philosophical insights? Marion seems to counsel great prudence in this regard.

Besides these more 'negative' insights, we have also already gained some more 'positive' pointers: speaking of God requires a different kind of language, a different mode of thinking, an opening of the heart rather than an expansion of the mind. It requires *addressing* God instead of merely speaking *about* God. The language that might be used of God is one of prayer, praise and devotion. While it is risky to speak about God, it is perfectly appropriate to speak *to* God. And doing so is not to abandon any attempt at rigorous thinking or knowledge altogether. Rather – and we will see this more fully soon – this alternative kind of thinking or knowing has its own rigour. It is not an abdication of thinking but its transformation into an entirely new dimension. Instead of a purely abstract or theoretical knowledge, it is an engaged kind of knowing, one of the heart or will. It is characterized by encounter and devotion rather than control or comprehension, thus bringing the theoretical and the practical together in unique ways. Marion begins to explicate this way of approaching God more fully in his juxtaposition of idol and icon.

Notes

1   *The Philosophical Writings of Descartes*, vol. 3, translated by John
    Cottingham, Robert Stoothoff, Dugald Murdoch and Anthony Kenny
    (Cambridge: Cambridge University Press, 1991), 23. Marion cites this
    phrase in many of his publications on Descartes. See, for example,
    his essay on the second part of the citation (EG, 103–15) or on its
    reception by Spinoza, Malebranche and Leibniz (EG, 116–38).

2   In her excellent *A Genealogy of Marion's Phenomenology of Religion:
    Apparent Darkness* (Bloomington: Indiana University Press, 2011)
    Tamsin Jones shows that things are considerably more complicated
    than that and that Marion often has recourse to Gregory of Nyssa's
    more developed theology on this point, while attributing some of
    Gregory's arguments to Dionysius and treating these early theologians
    fairly monolithically. A more careful distinction between their
    theologies and methods, Jones suggests, might actually have clarified
    Marion's own argument and made it ultimately more successful.
    Jones also provides a far more detailed discussion than I can give here
    of Marion's engagement with patristic texts and of his analysis of
    apophatic theology.

2

Approaching God

Marion is perhaps best known for his provocative *God without Being*, which was for a long time the only one of his books translated into English and so significantly (and somewhat misleadingly) shaped the debate of his work in English-language scholarship. The book grew out of a conference organized by Richard Kearney and Joseph O'Leary in Paris on the question of God in relation to Heidegger's work and in the wake of what has come to be called 'the death of God'. Marion had already been intensely interested in this question, arguing in *Idol and Distance* and several articles that the death of God is the death of a particular idolatrous version of the divine and ultimately implies 'the death of the death of God' and hence a new possibility for a more divine God to appear. He carries this discussion further in *God without Being* with the important distinction between the idol and the icon – two modes of approaching the divine. Here we are dealing not just with a language that might articulate something about God, but with a way of nearing God, with attempts to come close to the divine. Marion continues to use the language of idol and icon also in his phenomenological work. That employment has both important continuities with his earlier explication and some differences. This chapter will lay out the various stages of Marion's discussion of how to approach God (and to some extent the human other and even the self): (1) via material idols and icons; (2) via conceptual idols and icons; (3) via the idol or icon as the work of art; and (4) via the relation of idol and icon to the face of the other.

1. Material idols and icons

Although *Idol and Distance* was written before *God without Being*, I will begin here with the latter text because it lays out the distinction between idol and icon most clearly and most evenly (*Idol and Distance* focuses more heavily on the idol, *The Crossing of the Visible* focuses more exclusively on the icon, especially the second half of the work). Marion distinguishes idol and icon as two ways of seeing, two modes of aiming at the divine. He is quite emphatic that the idol is not somehow a 'false' or 'inauthentic' seeing, but rather a different way of seeing; its aim does not require censure (GWB, 13–15). The idol is the result of a vision of the divine that proceeds from the viewer or the one who worships. This person has seen many things that did not interest it, but the vision of the divine catches its gaze, stops it short, fascinates and dazzles it. The gaze is completely wrapped up in this vision; the idol fills the gaze entirely. It thus provides an exact measure of what the gaze can bear and functions as an invisible mirror; it is the exact match of the aim of that particular gaze. The idol invites the worship of its devotees, draws them to itself, because it corresponds exactly to their own desires and images of the divine. This is true also of 'secular' idols: the sports stars we adulate, the film stars we celebrate, the fashion idols we envy all represent exact images or mirrors of our own secret desires and dreams. The idol is hence not false, but eminently authentic; it presents a true mirror of our aim, fits us perfectly. It is the focus of *our* approach and admiration. Marion suggests that the 'idols' of the past as they are displayed in museums and exhibits no longer function as gods not because they were inauthentic or false versions of the divine, but because they no longer fascinate us. If new worshippers of such idols were to emerge, they would again become true idols, that is to say, genuine experiences of the divine (GWB, 27–8). A material idol, then, is the work of an artist who has had a vision of the divine and seeks to present this vision as exactly as possible, hence enabling others to approach the divine in similar fashion. The idol is a visible representation of what the religious artist has seen of the divine.

The icon functions in the reverse. In the case of the idol, the human gaze aims at the divine, is dazzled by its vision, filled by it and returned on itself. In the case of the icon, the gaze is stopped not by the icon itself, but by a gaze or aim behind the actual image. Instead of being reflected by the idol, the gaze itself becomes envisioned by the icon. Instead of gazing *at* the icon, *we* find ourselves being gazed at. The aim is suddenly directed at us, comes to us. We find ourselves exposed, examined, laid open and vulnerable. In material icons this is achieved via what is called 'inverse perspective': the vanishing point does not lie behind the image, as is the case in Western paintings since the Renaissance, creating the effect of three-dimensionality perceived from the standpoint of the observer, but instead the image is painted in such a way that this point lies in front of the image, turning the observer into the one observed – the gaze or aim proceeds from *behind* the icon. Mountains and buildings in the icon often seem to collapse toward the viewer and show three sides of the building simultaneously. This is not a bizarre distortion, but a deliberate reversal of the perspective, locating the aim of the view not in front of but inside or behind the icon. Marion uses this function of the icon to suggest that adoration of the icon here has been reversed; it is no longer a mirror image of my own desires, wishes and imaginations, but rather has opened me to *its* desires and wishes. Instead of staging an active approach that would be in control of the image, as is the case for the idol, a less active approach is required – one that is receptive to what is being given, what comes to us. The icon in some way maintains the invisibility of the divine.

Both idols and icons, then, function as ways of approaching the divine. But in one case the approach is on our terms, in the other case it is on God's terms. In one case our vision is imposed on the divine and the resulting idol is an expression of what we have seen. Or, as Marion says: 'In the idol the human experience of the divine precedes the face that that divinity assumes in it' (ID, 5). In the other case, the divine gaze crosses our gaze via the icon and what is 'seen' becomes a mere vehicle of what remains essentially invisible. Both are real material expressions of what it means to approach the divine; to some extent God becomes truly 'incarnate' in both. Both manifest God – or at least some aspect of the divine – but they do so in different ways. In the first case of the idol, the manifestation and its material expression are almost entirely grounded in the viewer and function as a measure of his or her capacity and desires. The primary concern of the manifestation is visibility. The artist attempts to render visible in paint or sculpture a particular vision of the divine. In the second case of the icon, the primary concern is to provide an approach that would maintain and protect invisibility. The manifestation and its material expression become a vehicle for a desire and capacity that always transcend the material manifestation and invite to continued exposure. The idol exposes the divine to the human and cuts the divine down to human measure; the icon exposes the human to the divine and opens the human up to the infinite divine without measure. The icon is infinitely excessive. In the case of the idol, the initiative for approaching God lies with the human. God becomes available to human experience, but within the measure and on the terms of the human. In the case of the icon, the initiative is shared: the approach finds itself at a crossroads and works in both directions. In the idol the divine takes on our features, while in the icon we are exposed to the face of the divine. The idol abolishes distance, while the icon preserves it.

2. Conceptual idols and icons

Marion contends that he is not merely describing particular material images or statues, although his analysis certainly also applies to them, but that idol and icon stand for two ways of approaching the divine, two modes of seeing and receiving. In both *God without Being* and *Idol and Distance*, he goes on to apply this analysis to more conceptual, less material versions of idols and icons. In *God without Being*, Marion moves quite quickly from discussing material idols and icons to considering how this distinction might apply on the more conceptual level. He argues that not just statues or images but concepts can also function as idols or icons, respectively. They can open up or close down an approach to God. Conceptual idols are ways of representing God that parallel images or other material representations. They function as idols by capturing the mental gaze, by dazzling it, filling it and returning it upon itself. Conceptual idols are concepts that once upon a time – and sometimes still – expressed exactly a person's or a society's vision of the divine or particular approach to God. Again, calling them idolatrous does not automatically or immediately invite censure. Rather, conceptual idols serve as modes of approaching God; these concepts function as invisible mirrors of the person or culture who formulates them, because they fill the gaze entirely, capture everything envisioned about God at that time and place, and consequently, in some sense, say more about the time and place than they do about God as such. But they are authentic, true conceptual expressions of an approach to 'God' that 'worked' and at that time in history and culture fulfil their function admirably.

Yet, such concepts are 'idolatrous' in the sense that they are *our* vision of God, our gaze aimed at God, our way of approaching God; they are in our control and ultimately in our image. And they equate the divine with a concept; God becomes determined by human speech and rationality. In this respect, they become outdated just like material idols; at some point they no longer invite worship, no longer represent our vision of the divine, no longer 'fit' what we have seen of God, no longer allow us to approach God. Conceptual idols can become obsolete, die with the visions that no longer capture the imagination, no longer move us, no longer seem 'right' for God, precisely because they fit a particular vision of 'God' and did not actually portray all – or possibly even very much – of God as such. In Marion's view, just as the history of cultures is full of obsolete idols that no longer arouse veneration, so the history of ideas is riddled with obsolete concepts of the divine that no longer express what we think to be true of God. In this sense, the philosophical critiques of concepts of God or the intellectual rejection of proofs for God's existence serve a useful function: they rid us of conceptual idols.

Marion gives concrete examples of such conceptual idols and in *Idol and Distance* even examines a whole history of successive conceptual idols that he identifies as metaphysical. To some extent a conceptual idol of God is always metaphysical, because it places certain restrictions on God, portrays the divine within certain predetermined boundaries. Indeed, Marion consistently identifies the idea of 'proving' God or God's existence with an idolatrous attempt at enclosing God in a concept or a conceptual construct. And all attempts to enclose or express God within a concept are ultimately metaphysical and culminate in atheism and nihilism. In colourful language Marion says that metaphysics as onto-theological atheism does not cease 'to force-feed us with ever more supreme beings' (ID, 18). Thus, although idolatrous concepts for the divine are not false inasmuch as they encapsulate a particular concept that seemed adequate at a specific point in history, they are far more dangerous than material idols and their abolishment or refutation is to be welcomed. The conceptual idol is like the univocal language or onto-theo-logical constitution examined in the previous chapter: God becomes dependent on us and our vision or conceptual tools. In the conceptual idol God takes on whatever features we decide to impose on the divine. It designates our experience of the divine, our creation. Turning Nietzsche's announcement on its head, Marion says that 'seeing' God via the idol ultimately means to kill the divine. Any philosophical definition of God usually functions as such a conceptual idol, whether this is Plato's idea of the good, Aristotle's unmoved mover, Descartes' causa sui, Leibniz' principle of sufficient reason, and so forth. Marion examines three versions of idolatrous concepts in more detail in various texts: those of Kant, Nietzsche and Heidegger. In each case, a previous version of a conceptual idol is overcome or demolished and a new version instituted.

Kant very effectively demolishes what he considered the idolatrous portrayals of the medieval and early modern period. He refutes all versions of proofs for God's existence with which he was familiar and insists that God is not accessible via human rationality. God does not fit into the conceptual apparatus that governs human understanding. We must thus suspend any judgement about the eternity or creation of the world, the immortality or death of the soul, and God's existence. Again, it is important to stress that Marion *applauds* this move. Kant's refutation of the proofs for God's existence rids us of metaphysical idols. Yet, Kant furnishes a new concept of God: that of the moral God. While theoretical reason has no access to the divine and can know nothing about God, practical reason has to posit the hypothesis of a God who rewards good deeds with happiness and is ultimately able to bring about a 'kingdom of ends' in order to assure a moral universe and the categorical imperative. This moral author of the world indeed refers to a genuine experience of the divine, but it is also again a limiting determination (GWB, 31–2).

This 'moral God' is challenged and demolished by Nietzsche's 'devaluation of all values'. Nietzsche shows that the concept of the moral god is an idolatrous one that is arbitrary and invalid. Morality consists in the will to power, not in a divine grounding of the categorical imperative. When Nietzsche's madman announces the death of god, it is the god of metaphysics, the god of Kant's moral universe, the god of the Platonic realm of the forms that is killed. It is thus not God as such who is overcome and made obsolete by Nietzsche, but a metaphysical idol of god. Thus, the death of god is actually good news, because it concerns the death of a particular version of god, an idolatrous version in which we no longer believe anyway. Marion often returns to this announcement of God's death. Sometimes he comments that any 'god' who can die cannot possibly ever have been a real God, thus pointing to the weakness and insufficiency of the concept of 'god' at work in this parable and the cultural reality it represents (ID, 3). At other times, he focuses more on it as an occasion for celebration, as the successful elimination of a constricting, metaphysical, idolatrous notion of the divine that we should be glad to witness being swept aside.

Marion claims that although Nietzsche rids us of the idol of the moral god and the metaphysical idolatry associated with a Platonic version of Christianity, he goes on to announce the coming of new gods. The revaluation of all values via the will to power leads to new versions of idolatry. The will to power itself emerges as a metaphysical construct that grounds a particular conceptual vision of reality, namely that of the eternal return. Nietzsche does not maintain the kind of distance that would be required in order not to turn God into an idol. Marion suggests that Heidegger's 'deconstruction of metaphysics' helps us escape this particular version of conceptual idolatry. Again, this destruction is therefore productive; it rids us of concepts that functioned idolatrously and are no longer appropriate. Yet, in Marion's view, Heidegger ultimately is unable to accomplish this step out of metaphysics entirely and becomes wrapped up in a second or doubled idolatry that is actually more dangerous than the earlier versions because it is so subtle and so close to us (GWB, 37). How is Heidegger still idolatrous? Marion contends that the 'gods' Heidegger introduces, especially in the notion of the fourfold, make god dependent on Being. In some sense Heidegger does exactly what happened at the time of Descartes and what Heidegger censures as onto-theo-logy: God becomes a being, maybe the supreme being (though probably not), but certainly one being among others. God becomes dependent on Dasein, on human conceptions of the divine. Within Heidegger's notion of the fourfold of heaven, earth, gods and mortals, the gods are one type of being among others, all dependent on Being as such (GWB, 37–49). In Marion's view, God cannot and should not be inscribed within ontological difference, if we are talking about God as such and not just a conceptual idol of god. This idolatrous approach to god must be overcome not with a new idol, but with an iconic approach to the divine.

An iconic vision or concept of God instead reverses and corrects the gaze. It proceeds from God toward the human gaze. The icon maintains that God is unthinkable and that no conditions or limits can be imposed on the divine. Marion already in these early texts equates the logic of the icon with that of the gift or of love – two themes that will grow increasingly more prominent in his work. The logic of the icon is one of abandon, of a kenotic giving. The icon, then, is not merely a particular concept or even a mode of being of the divine, but it denotes activity and relation. As Marion says, 'love is not spoken but made' (GWB, 107). In *God without Being*, Marion proposes such an iconic approach via a reading of several biblical passages that seem to suspend 'being' in some form or other (Rom. 4.17, 1 Cor. 1.28, Luke 15.12-32). For example, in the parable of the prodigal son, the errant son asks for the father's *ousia* (usually translated as 'inheritance' but in Greek the same term as that used for 'being' or 'essence' and which Marion reads in light of Heidegger's concept of Being as such). Thus, the son defines the father in terms of the essence or being or things he may derive from him; he thinks of the father as a property, as something having cash value, as an object of transaction. When the son returns, the father instead receives him with forgiveness and generosity, invalidating the logic of property and retribution. The father invalidates the logic of *ousia* – of essence or property – via the logic of the abundant gift of his love. Similarly, in a text in the first letter to the Corinthians, Paul talks about the believers in Corinth as ones who counted for nothing in the eyes of the world, had no 'being' in terms of worldly estimation, but who are given value by the gratuitous gift of God's love. The worldly logic of being and status is overturned by the logic of love and redemption.

Marion speaks of this as an undoing of metaphysics that does not take it directly, but rather sideways. It invalidates the logic of ontological difference by being 'indifferent' to it or by 'outwitting' it 'at its own game' (GWB, 84). Marion argues that Heidegger,

despite his occasional separation of 'God' and 'Being' (as in the
pronouncement that if he ever were to write a theology the word
'being' would not appear in it, or his consistent insistence that
'Being' is not another term for God), still makes God subject
to and dependent upon Being and 'Being' remains the highest
name or most elevated concern in his work. Phenomenology, as
Heidegger's *Being and Time* lays out in great detail and his essay
'Phenomenology and Theology' explicitly maintains, is the most
fundamental investigation; all others, including theology, are mere
'regional' or partial disciplines or investigations. For Heidegger,
phenomenology examines the being of the human being as such,
while theology is only concerned with the particular situation
of a believing human being and examines that human being's
faith. Theology is then a limited and particular concern, while
phenomenology in Heidegger's eyes addresses what is truly fundamental and primordial. By showing that this (phenomenological)
concern with being can on occasion be set aside or rendered
irrelevant by theological instances, Marion wants to demonstrate
that it is precisely *not* the most fundamental or only concern, as
Heidegger seems to claim, but that other concerns, such as love,
touch us much more deeply and more profoundly and ultimately
matter more.

Marion actually works this out more fully in a chapter on 'vanity'
– here designating not pride but meaninglessness or pointlessness,
as in Ecclesiastes: 'All is vanity' (GWB, 108–38). Vanity constitutes
to some extent a transitional moment between idol and icon. In the
case of the idol, we are 'hooked', fully engaged, completely dazzled.
The case of vanity is the reverse: everything leaves us cold or indifferent, we are bored stiff, uninterested, nothing matters any more.
Heidegger had already investigated the mood of boredom and the
ways in which it dissolves our commitment to being or distracts
us from ontological difference (at least in Marion's interpretation).
Vanity goes even further. It is superlative indifference and touches
everything with meaninglessness or 'caducity' – making it obsolete,
empty, null and void. The experience of 'vanity' thus severs our
relation to being; being becomes superfluous, a nothing, a void.
As the ancient sin of 'acedia' or the illness of 'melancholia', vanity
has no room for love or interest of any sort. It suspends being as a
concern and shows that it is not most fundamental or primordial.
Ultimately, Marion suggests, it shows that it matters more to us

whether we are loved and are of importance to someone than whether we exist. And love functions in some way as the reverse of vanity: in its case also, being does not matter, because only the place and time I spend with my beloved is of concern to me. All other concerns are effectively set aside and rendered meaningless; I am indifferent to them and only occupied with what or whom I love.

In *Idol and Distance* the link between the idol and metaphysics in relation to Nietzsche and Heidegger is even stronger, albeit explicated somewhat differently. The very point of this early text was an attempt to get beyond or even 'destroy' metaphysics, which Marion here closely identifies with Heidegger's notion of ontological difference, again employing Heidegger's definition of metaphysics as onto-theo-logy to work out what metaphysics means and how it is to be 'overcome'. Instead of ontological difference, Marion seeks to elaborate a notion of distance he considers more appropriate for the divine. Distance must be maintained and crossed, rather than erased or ignored. We approach God only by traversing distance rather than eliminating it. Three figures help Marion articulate progressively more successful formulations of distance: Nietzsche, Hölderlin and Dionysius the Areopagite. In the first chapter Marion works out Nietzsche's replacement of the Kantian conceptual idol of the moral god. As already indicated above, he stresses that the notion of the death of god is productive and helpful, even an occasion for celebration, because it is the death of a very particular god, a metaphysical idol of the divine. We should be glad to be rid of it and grateful to Nietzsche for accomplishing it. Yet, Nietzsche does not go far enough. He introduces new idols, hence new gods, and especially the will to power that reinstitutes metaphysics. Ultimately, 'the Nietzschean distance intervenes only to censure the distance of God, or more, to obliterate it, within the evidence of the text, by substituting itself for it' (ID, 77).

Hölderlin goes further. Marion examines his poetry, especially some of the more explicitly religious poems such as 'In Lovely Blue', 'The Only One' or 'Patmos'. Hölderlin indicates a measure of divine withdrawal in his poetic imagery by designating Christ as the only one and emphasizing the divine distance expressed in poverty, suffering and even some allusions to the Eucharist (especially in the poem 'Bread and Wine'). Although Marion sees Hölderlin's poetry as providing significant insight on trinitarian distance by thinking poetically through the mystery of the father as a kind of kenotic withdrawal, Marion admits that such insight only comes with certain presuppositions when reading the texts. Their poetic nature allows for many other readings: while Christ is identified as 'the only one', he also becomes absorbed into our 'carnal love' and our habitat (ID, 117) and ultimately the 'withdrawal of the Father' and the 'retreat of the gods' are indistinguishable (ID, 137). Hölderlin's silence on the divine cannot be clearly identified as iconic, but may well continue to be idolatrous. Therefore, as we already saw in the previous chapter, Marion goes on to posit Dionysius as an alternative to Nietzsche and Hölderlin. Dionysius is able to articulate a version of distance that does not fall into the metaphysical traps of ontological difference. His version of the divine hierarchy maintains the requisite distance between the divine and the human and hence allows us to approach God by crossing distance without erasing it or forgetting it, but continually maintaining it. Thus, this use of Dionysius is not only about appropriate language for God, but also indicates how God might be approached. And Marion does briefly employ the language of the icon here already. As icon of the invisible God, Christ mediates the divine not by providing a reproduction of God, but by communicating the divine to us. The 'hierarchy functions then as an icon of the Trinity' (ID, 176). It is possible to participate in the divine, and in the process receive ourselves, by maintaining the proper distance.

The distance that Marion attempts to articulate in *Idol and Distance* is ultimately about relation: both inter-trinitarian relation, such as the relation between Father and Son, and relation between the divine and the human. To approach God iconically means to traverse that distance without erasing it, to approach the divine while continually keeping in mind (and practice) God's utter alterity. Yet, at the same time, it is about God's approach to us, especially as it is exemplified in the incarnation and supremely in Christ's death on the cross. Marion says repeatedly that we 'see' God's invisibility in Christ's wounds (ID, 113; PC, 11, 67). The 'folly' of the cross is also the 'logos' or rationality of the cross, which is the logic of the icon. This logic is one of gift, abandonment, self-giving, suffering – in short, a logic of agapic love. God is revealed in the withdrawal and advent that characterizes the incarnation and the crucifixion. God must be 'crossed out' in order to be approached adequately. It is hence, as Marion reiterates several times, not a matter of

'knowing' God but of loving or receiving the divine. Only thus can
we be freed from idolatry.

3. The idol or icon as work of art

Already in *God without Being* the initial discussion of idol and
icon had some connections to art. The material portrayal of the
god by a religious artist, often thereafter displayed in museums,
we now mostly think of as an artistic rendering, even if its initial
aim was solely to make visible the vision of the divine. On the
very first page of *God without Being*, Marion refers to idol and
icon as works of art, or in fact 'two models of art' (GWB, 1). In
his explicitly phenomenological work Marion later re-introduces
the notions of idol and icon, but there they function phenomenologically to designate particular experiences. The idol has lost
almost all connections to the divine and stands primarily for the
experience of a work of art, especially that of a painting, a topic
on which Marion has written extensively. (Although Marion very
occasionally mentions music and sometimes considers other works
of art, his main focus is always on painting.) Yet despite this development of the notion of the idol, it has many continuities with
the earlier account. The phenomenological idol is what dazzles
the gaze, what fills it with the brilliance of the visible. It shows
the visible in its full glory and, in fact, gives everything to be seen.
It is a full manifestation of visibility in its most intensive degree.
Marion draws a distinction between 'seeing' and 'appearing': while
we may well see any number of things, they only appear to us when
we pay attention to them. We see objects, but paintings appear to
us. They have an effect on us, draw us to themselves. Paintings
have their own logic, their own rigour, their own right(s). Aesthetic
experience is thus an immensely rich and important domain that,
Marion suggests, deserves much fuller exploration than it has
received so far and can also make a significant phenomenological
contribution.

Like the earlier discussion of the idol, the phenomenological idol
as work of art shows precisely what a gaze can bear – both the
gaze of the painter who originally created the painting as a representation of a vision of the unseen and the gaze of the observer

who accesses this vision via the painting. Marion says that 'my idol defines what I can bear of phenomenality – the maximum of intuitive intensity that I can endure while keeping my look on a distinctly visible spectacle'. As in the case of the religious idol, the phenomenological idol 'exposes the span of all my aims – what I set my heart on seeing, and thus also what I want to see and do'. Therefore, 'what I admire judges me' (IE, 61). This is true not only of the observer. Marion suggests that painters have an experience of the realm of the unseen, discover a previously unseen phenomenon, and then try to 'translate' it into visibility in order to allow others to access this vision as well. Indeed, through painting the artist actually makes new phenomena, introduces new 'visibles' into the world (IE, 69). In his chapter on painting in *In Excess*, Marion focuses on abstract art, especially that of Mark Rothko and Paul Klee, to show how it conveys a particular kind of experience. The painter conveys this phenomenon into full visibility into a dazzling representation of his or her own vision. The work of art, like the idol, calls for adoration or veneration: we must return to see a great painting again and again (IE, 71, 74). Seeing it only once, or even analysing its physical or material features, is completely insufficient for experiencing its excessive visibility. The painting calls us to itself, in order to experience its overwhelming visibility.

Although Marion's analysis of the phenomenological idol is primarily about painting and the work of art more generally and says very little about God or a possible religious dimension to this phenomenon, the parallels to his more explicitly religious work are striking. The painting is a 'revelation' and clearly has a connotation of the sacred. Indeed, in many contexts Marion's descriptions of the phenomenon of painting or art are indistinguishable from those of revelation or an experience of the divine. He even uses exactly the same language to speak of the role of the theologian or philosopher of religion as he does of that of the painter. Just as the painter has experienced a phenomenon in the realm of the unseen and then expresses it via a work of art, translating it into the realm of the visible, so the theologian has experienced a phenomenon in the realm of the third order – that of charity, formulates it conceptually with philosophical tools, and hence translates it into the second order where it becomes much more widely accessible (VR, 74). An earlier text makes these parallels particularly obvious. *The Crossing of the Visible* takes up the same distinction between idol and icon articulated in *Idol and Distance* or *God without Being*, but here applies it to paintings and actual religious icons. Unlike the later phenomenological texts, however, the theological implications are present throughout and worked out much more fully.

As later in *In Excess* and 'What We See and What Appears', Marion argues in *The Crossing of the Visible* that painting makes visible what was previously unseen: the vision of a particular artist who renders into visibility what has captivated him or her, usually in the form of a painting or work of art, so that others might also be fascinated and dazzled by it, might have access to the painter's vision. Painters are those who have experienced or approached something in the realm of the unseen; one might say that they have had a kind of vision. They are so captivated by this vision that they seek to represent what they have discovered, to transfer it from the realm of the unseen to the world of the visible. Indeed, according to Marion one can distinguish between authentic and inauthentic paintings by the extent to which the artists make the unseen visible in the painting. Their rendering of the unseen in visibility is a measure of their ability to bear up under the weight of the unseen. The work of art, especially painting, is the visible manifestation of the previously unseen reality, captured in the artists' vision and expressed via their execution and production of the work. The unseen is not the same as the invisible; the invisible remains invisible (in the icon), the unseen is able to become at least partially visible (in the idol). But no censure of art is implied here. Marion defines the genius as someone who is able to bear the weight of the unseen, who holds up under it, who can carry what it imposes and is able to render it in visible form, hence making it accessible to everyone else – or at least to everyone capable of being dazzled and captured by the resulting work (IE, 51–2).

In the first chapter of *The Crossing of the Visible*, Marion engages in a detailed analysis of perspective in painting and the ways in which visible and invisible interact within it. He argues that a painting actually renders an experience of consciousness. The use of perspective makes real the visible via the invisible (what is not seen in the painting) and gives it to the aim of the viewer. The icon, in contrast, makes real the invisible via the visible and by refusing perspective (or inverting it) exposes the viewer to an aim proceeding from the icon. In it, the 'invisible is received but not produced' (CV, 23). And already in the analysis of painting itself, long before he moves to discussing the religious icon, Marion uses heavily religious terminology and frequently makes religious allusions. Paintings participate in a resurrection (CV, 27). They are 'sanctified', 'consecrated' or 'hallowed' (CV, 28). Paintings are 'graced' and participate in the 'creation' (CV, 29). The weight bearing on the artist is a measure of its 'glory' (the Hebrew word for 'glory' also means weight) and imposes a moral responsibility. The painting shows the 'stigmata of the unseen' (CV, 37) and is able to render the unexpected, unthinkable and impossible visible in its dazzling radiance. Here the painting and the painter in many ways function as an indication of the sacred or even as a sort of Christ figure. True paintings open 'the gates of Hell' and their glory makes the light dawn (CV, 29). Paintings work miracles and trace the very trembling of the earth. Paintings teach us to see what is given and help us to welcome it. The painter, then, has a quasi-religious task of rendering the sacred accessible to others.

In the third essay, Marion censures the status of the image in the contemporary media culture and its detrimental effects on our perceptions of ourselves. Here he speaks of images as idols with a more negative connotation, arguing that they are indicative of the nihilism of our culture. To the secular image he contrasts the religious icon, in this context interacting explicitly with some of the texts written in defence of icons during the iconoclastic period in the Christian East. The icon does not attract attention to itself – unlike the idol – but defers it to the one it is meant to represent. As John of Damascus and Theodore the Studite argue, veneration of the icon is not directed at the material image but ascends to its 'prototype': Christ or the saint portrayed in the image. These thinkers also make an important distinction between worship or adoration (*latreia*) and veneration (*proskuneisis*). Only God is worshipped; icons are venerated. They are vehicles for adoration, means for approaching the divine, not the end in themselves. One approaches God by going through them and exposing oneself to the divine in prayer. The icon uses visibility in such a way that it protects the invisible, but allows for the 'crossing of gazes' across it. The icon is a 'kenosis of the image' (CV, 63) that allows a trace of God to emerge via the face of Christ portrayed on the icon. The icon serves as a 'recording' of these traces (CV, 75). As in *God without Being* and in the first chapter of *Prolegomena to Charity*, the invisible only becomes visible in Christ's wounds (CV, 74), in the marks of the nails on the cross.

Marion here equates holiness with kenosis (CV, 76). Holiness becomes visible only in self-renunciation and the supreme self-sacrifice on the cross. While the idol displays glory in abundance and exalts in self-glorification, the icon returns all glory to the invisible. Christ is the icon of the invisible God because his human death on the cross simultaneously shows his divinity: 'the mortal sufferings of the invisible holiness in the horror of the visible sin' (CV, 84). We see God in Christ via the Spirit in the distance of the cross and the relation between visible and invisible that the icon attempts to portray. The icon must always have a trinitarian basis, which alone enables it to maintain the fragile balance between distance and advent, presence and absence, visible and invisible. As the Father is given in love in the Son and the love between Father and Son communicated by the Spirit, so the icon attempts to express the same perichoretic relation, now opening us to this divine gift of love. This happens not only in the material icon, as it portrays an image of Christ, but more profoundly within the liturgy where all the senses are exposed and attuned to the divine gift of Christ's body (CV, 64). While to an idolatrous gaze the liturgy may seem a mere spectacle, someone exposed to the crossing of the visible by the invisible in prayer experiences the liturgy as the gift of God's love. We will return to the theological implications of this discussion in a moment, but let me complete the picture with a brief analysis of Marion's use of the icon in his phenomenological work.

4. Idol and icon as face of the other

Marion had already made the link between the icon and the face in *God without Being* (GWB, 19). The notion of the icon also becomes re-employed in Marion's phenomenology of givenness (which will be laid out in more detail in the next chapter). Its function remains essentially the same as in the earlier expositions, although, as in the case of the idol, the content changes. The icon still designates the counter-gaze who envisions me, comes to me, aims at me, but it is now primarily the gaze of the human other rather than that of the divine. Marion certainly never suggests that this analysis would *not* apply to the gaze of the divine other, but it is no longer the focus of his discussion. While the idol as work of art dazzles the gaze with its intense quality, the icon returns the gaze upon itself. It designates the experience of being envisioned by the other, of having the other come to me. I approach the idol, indeed must go to see it again and again, so mesmerized am I by its overwhelming brilliance, while I respond to the prior gaze of the icon, expose myself to its view, receive what it grants me. Neither can be controlled or mastered, both have to be received at least to some extent, yet the mode of approach and reception is quite different. I 'see' nothing in the case of the icon, except maybe the emptiness of the other's pupils. Marion previews this to some extent in an early chapter on love in *Prolegomena to Charity*, where he is especially in dialogue with Lévinas, but works it out more fully in Chapter 5 of *In Excess*. As I will deal with Marion's phenomenology more fully in the following chapter, I will focus here only on the aspects relevant to the notion of the icon per se and the ways in which this discussion adds to what we have seen in the earlier treatments.

Like the religious icon, the phenomenological category of the icon reverses the gaze and gives rise to a 'counter-intentionality' (IE, 113). Instead of looking at the face, I experience it and become a witness to it. The face remains invisible. Indeed, the only way to protect its phenomenality as a face is through maintaining its invisibility and incomprehensibility. Here Marion is deeply influenced by Lévinas' account of the face and of alterity: the otherness of the other remains inviolable, to know or grasp the face is to kill it. Not only the flesh of the other person remains inaccessible to me, as Husserl pointed out, but the other's face, encapsulated in the other's gaze, is invisible: I do not look at the other's features but fix on the 'empty pupils of the person's eyes', thus 'on the sole place where precisely nothing can be seen' (IE, 115). The face is not given as a spectacle, but speaks to us – and even that not always in comprehensible or logical speech but instead via the injunction 'Thou shalt not kill!' And even killing the other does not ultimately give me access to or power over the other's face. The other as other cannot be grasped. Any attempt to do so would turn the human into an object and thereby precisely have missed what is human about the face. The face says, as Christ does to Mary on the morning of the resurrection: 'noli me tangere'; do not touch me (IE, 117). Marion seeks to free this Lévinasian injunction from its ethical parameters and to widen it to any call coming from the face: for example, an existential or an erotic one. Like the icon, the face aims at me, takes me in view, makes 'the weight of its glory' descend on me, 'because I feel myself called and held at a distance by the weight of an invisible look, by its silent appeal' (IE, 119). It is worth pointing out that Marion mentions this inviolability of the face already in his discussion of the idol in the third chapter of *In Excess*. Art has a responsibility for what it portrays and the kind of effect it seeks to produce. In this context, Marion suggests that the painting of faces is particularly fraught with moral dangers, because the face is the domain of the icon, while painting is concerned with the idol (IE, 76–9). Rothko did not paint faces, precisely out of a recognition and acknowledgement of this moral dimension and in order to honour it (IE, 78). The face can never be given to full visibility. It is interesting that Marion's analyses of art have a strongly ethical tenor in a way that is without parallel in the rest of his work, which generally leaves the topic of ethics aside. He censures Rothko's Houston chapel, implying that it has no space for the sacred sacrament because it erases the divine face through the artwork. Works of art are uniquely incarnate and bear the profound responsibility for their transfer of phenomena from the realm of the unseen to the realm of visibility. Only 'great' works of art can do this successfully and it takes genius to perform it well. Mediocre art is a quasi-moral failure, albeit a very common one. Marion reiterates this moral responsibility of the artist in other places.

In the later chapter on the icon, however, Marion explicitly seeks to broaden the analysis of the icon as face beyond its religious connotations and beyond the ethical ones it has for Lévinas and of which he warns us in his work on art. Instead, he reads the icon primarily as a reversal of gazes in more general terms. While the structure of the phenomenological icon remains the same (exposure to a gaze that aims at me, experience of an invisible weight bearing upon me), its content is no longer concerned with the divine but instead entirely with the human gaze. Yet, this transition is itself revealing and points to certain parallels between human and divine other, which Marion has explicated more fully in his more recent work. In the discussion within *In Excess* he only briefly returns to some religious implications at the end of the chapter, but these already are telling: the face as icon is infinitely incomprehensible;

my inability to understand or grasp the other is not a lack or an error, but rather a way of protecting and safeguarding the other's inviolability; the infinity of the other requires a fidelity that goes all the way to death or even beyond. And such fidelity to the other requires an 'infinite hermeneutics', a ceaselessly varied interpretation, which can only be accomplished if one believes in immortality and leaves the last judgement to God (IE, 123). While the face always remains inaccessible for phenomenology, theology or faith believe in the 'manifestation of the face of the other person' in the 'return of Christ' because the glory of the human face is ultimately an indication of the infinite face of God (IE, 124). The infinity of the face calls for a belief in immortality; we must live 'as if' holiness were possible in an infinite progress toward greater freedom that continues beyond death. Even to do justice to the memory of the other and to mourn appropriately by bearing witness to the other's infinity 'compels me to believe in my own eternity, like a need of reason, or, what comes down to the same thing, as the condition of the infinite hermeneutic' of the other (IE, 127).

Marion extends this discussion of the human as incomprehensible and indefinable in the first chapter of *Negative Certainties*. He shows how various experiences turn humans into objects: being a patient at a hospital, being an immigrant or a stateless person, becoming a mere statistic in economic analysis. All these are inappropriate ways of speaking of the human. They alienate us from ourselves and miss what is at stake in humanity. Marion grounds this again in the analysis of the face. And, as he points out here, it is not only the other we cannot comprehend or know, it is also the self. I am not a thing (even a 'thinking thing', as Descartes had called us) or a substance or a 'transcendental unity of apperception' (as Kant had claimed). Marion cites Augustine, who maintained that 'I remain a question to myself' (NC, 15). The human is inaccessible to the self and irreducible to any definition (NC, 16). The human is unknowable in principle; this essential unknowability is precisely what distinguishes us as human in Marion's view. But it distinguishes us from objects, not necessarily from God. Marion explicitly appeals to the theological idea of the human being created in the image of God to support this. Like God, the human cannot be known and cannot be reduced to an object or even a being. As being is not the central question for God, so it is also not the central concern for the human. Marion quotes Gregory of Nyssa, who explains the nature of the icon as pointing to what exceeds comprehension and then speaks of the human as an icon of the creator that escapes comprehension and hence is similar to God (NC, 32). To know humans is to refer them back to the incomprehensible God. Marion cites several other patristic and medieval thinkers who establish such a parallel and deduce the incomprehensibility of the human from it. Humans are as incomprehensible and indefinable as the divine.

And this is perfectly consistent with comments Marion makes elsewhere. The human, he says, is a 'god' in the way in which a painting by Cézanne can be said to be 'a Cézanne' – not identical to the painter but recognizable as created by him and in some way bearing his uniqueness (CpV, 123; SP, 256; NC, 41). The human must be acknowledged as a 'God' in this way (NC, 41). This is a derived name, however: while the human (Adam) can name the animals, he cannot name himself or God. They remain inaccessible and indefinable. Only God can name us. The human face cannot be imaged (not even in a painting) but is in the image of God. And to be in the image of God is to be – like Christ – an icon of God, an icon of the invisible (CV, 77). To be genuinely human is to allow the divine invisibility to become visible in our flesh, to allow the divine artisan to paint an icon on our creatureliness. The divine and the human hence become closely linked for Marion. What we can say about the human, although maybe inspired by Lévinas' phenomenology of alterity, is parallel to and rooted in what we can know about Christ. Hence although the language of icon apparently moves away from an approach to the divine and becomes focused entirely on the human other, the structural similarities ensure that human and divine other function in the same way. The other is approached as icon if he or she is approached as an icon of God.

Thus, while the desire to overcome metaphysics still plays a significant role in Marion's analysis of idol and icon, he is focused much more on a kind of advance or approach to God (and even the human) rather than just providing a reflection about appropriate and inappropriate language for the divine. There are, of course, significant parallels. On the one hand, God's transcendence is to be preserved in this approach and any vision of the divine that is dependent on the human gaze is limited by it and becomes idolatrous. Although it is an 'authentic' and genuine vision of the divine, it ultimately functions as a mirror only of one's own desires and aims. Instead God must be approached in such a way as to expose oneself to the divine gaze and to be open to a radical reorientation. On the other hand, as in the work on Descartes, there are also indications in the analysis of idol and icon that prayer, gift and love will play important roles in encountering the divine. We approach the divine by praying before the icon and it is the language of gift and love that undoes the idolatrous language of being. These latter indications especially will have to be worked out more fully in Marion's subsequent work. Beyond these parallels, there are also new insights. Although idol and icon can indeed be juxtaposed as an inappropriate and a more appropriate way of approaching the divine, there is also a sense in which they may be said to be two aspects of the same move, especially in the more recent work. Approaching God has two essentially connected dimensions: it means to be dazzled by an overwhelming vision, but also to be exposed to an invisible gaze. In one sense, God comes to us in overwhelming plenitude and full immanence; in the other sense, God's transcendence is preserved via apophatic absence and distance. The abundant vision of God overwhelms us with its immensity and grandeur, but it also blinds us, calls us out of ourselves, unsettles us, reorients us; it gives us nothing visible or tangible but instead calls us beyond ourselves. In some ways, we must approach in fear and trembling and must learn to bear the abundance of the given. At the same time, that means to approach empty, with open hands, ready to expose ourselves to the divine gaze. While in the earliest explications of the idol, the first aspect is still associated with an inadequate, albeit authentic, vision of the divine, one that is dependent upon the human gaze directed toward it, especially in Marion's work on art it increasingly becomes a way of bearing the impact of what is imposed on the gaze and rendering it faithfully. Such an approach characterizes not only the artist but also the theologian. We will return to this more fully in Chapter 4, but will now turn to a more detailed explication of what it might mean to experience God – not just to approach, but to enter wholly into the experience of the phenomenon.

3

Experiencing God

Phenomenology studies human experience. Husserl, often called the father of phenomenology, focused on the experience of consciousness, as it is constituted by the transcendental subject through various noetic acts. That is to say, instead of being concerned about the relationship between empirical objects 'out there' and their projected images inside the mind – as was true for much of modern philosophy – Husserl set aside or 'bracketed' these questions about the existence of objects 'out there' and instead focused on what actually appears to consciousness in order to analyse how we experience phenomena. By carefully examining phenomena as they actually appear to us, we can perceive patterns and structures that allow us to constitute them and to get to their essence or form; in other words, we are not concerned merely with personal, subjective experience, but with the structures of human experience more generally (just as a scientist is not interested in one particular fruit fly's behaviour but is trying to establish more general rules or patterns regarding reproduction or the transmission of genes). The process of 'bracketing' or setting aside certain beliefs or concerns about the world in order to focus more fully on what appears is called the *epoché* or the reduction (Husserl distinguishes between several types of reduction, but Marion generally speaks only of *the* reduction). The 'transcendental ego' (or 'transcendental subject') is the consciousness that brings together the insights of examination resulting from the reduction and is hence able to constitute the phenomenon as a whole; it is not a personal, subjective self having a particular empirical and entirely arbitrary experience.

The phenomenon is constituted from the 'noematic' content given via intuition – in other words, what is actually perceived or experienced of the phenomenon. The phenomenon also has 'noetic' aspects, which distinguish whether it is experienced as a memory, an imagination, an observation, and so forth. Furthermore, phenomena always appear within a horizon. We do not perceive 'red' in the abstract, but the red of the ladybug that has landed on the window sill or of the autumn leaves scattered on the green lawn. Phenomena appear to us within a context and the context is part of the experience of the phenomenon. Yet, even in attentive examination of what appears and how it appears, aspects of the phenomenon are always hidden. We don't see the back of an object or what is underneath it. When we walk around it or pick it up, other aspects of the object become invisible. It is impossible to perceive the entire object at once. We supply these other aspects through intentionality, we 'intend' (or 'apperceive') the back or underside. By varying the appearance of the thing in memory, imagination or judgement, we are able to constitute the phenomenon as a whole, rather than just what we can intuit at a particular moment or from a specific limited perspective.

Husserl's phenomenology is considerably more complex than this and also went through multiple versions as he continued revising his project (and often changed terminology). Subsequent phenomenologists also introduced changes or carried aspects of his thought further in novel ways. But this brief summary may serve as a starting point for making sense of what Marion is doing, both in terms of his reliance on Husserl and his criticism of aspects of the phenomenological project. Marion thinks of phenomenology as a progressive endeavour that is continued by each new generation of phenomenologists, who despite all their at times harsh critique, do not invalidate the insights of earlier thinkers but rather rely on them, carry them further and add to them in productive ways (RC, 120–1). Phenomenology is a joint project that works on 'the things themselves', on phenomena as they give themselves to us. The task of phenomenology is to be as faithful to phenomena as possible and to describe them as carefully as can be done. I will first present (1) the notion of givenness, absolutely central to Marion's project, then (2) his proposal of what he calls 'saturated phenomena', and especially (3) the saturated phenomenon of revelation. The chapter will conclude with the most recent notion Marion has advanced for phenomenology, namely (4) the idea of 'negative certainties'. The notion of the gift, closely connected to the phenomenology of givenness and also an important topic in Marion's work, will be considered in the subsequent chapter.

1. Givenness

The language of givenness is central to Marion's phenomenological project and maybe its most defining feature. Husserl already had spoken of the *Gegebenheit* of phenomena, which could be translated as their being present, taking place, or being given, but etymologically speaking *gegeben* does indeed mean 'given'. Translating it as *donation* into French and *givenness* into English, however, seems to imply that someone is doing the giving of the phenomenon (at least it implies it more than other more neutral translations) and so there has been some controversy over the translation (which will not concern us here, as this is an introduction to Marion's thought, not an evaluation of its level of faithfulness to one of the myriad interpretations of Husserl's phenomenological project; he addresses the objections in BG, 61–4; IE, 21–3 and even more fully in the first two essays in *The Reason of the Gift*). More importantly, Marion claims that previous phenomenologists had not been sufficiently faithful to the basic phenomenological call to return to the things themselves as they actually appear. Husserl, so Marion contends, was concerned primarily with the constitution of objects. All the phenomena he examines are objects, which are experienced by a transcendental subject. This subject is to a large extent in control of them, because it constitutes them as objects via intentionality. Marion suggests that this imposes parameters and constrictions on these phenomena, especially by turning them into objects and making them depend on the constitution of the subject. The 'things' are no longer able to appear on their own terms. They are always confined to being objects and examined only in terms of their 'objectness' (a term Marion prefers to 'objectivity' in order to be able to distinguish between Husserl's *Gegenständlichkeit* and *Objektivität*).

Marion is obviously not the only one to have noticed this somewhat restrictive scope of Husserlian phenomenology.

Heidegger already expanded (some would say subverted) the Husserlian project to provide a different account of our being in the world and our experience of the world, each other and ourselves. As we have already seen in earlier chapters, the question of being is central for Heidegger and one he thinks has been neglected by the tradition, which is only concerned in various ways with particular beings and not with Being *per se*. It has forgotten this ontological difference, eliding the difference between beings and Being, between being and beingness. Heidegger speaks of the being who examines its own being as *Dasein* and provides an extensive analysis of how Dasein experiences itself and its world, focusing far more explicitly than Husserl on moods, emotions, fears, and what might be called more interior experiences rather than experiences of objects (although Heidegger also provides a famous analysis of our use of tools, such as a hammer, which ironically appears to us more fully when it is missing or when we hit our finger instead of the nail, rather than when we use it unthinkingly and automatically). Marion thinks that Heidegger's phenomenology is an important step forward, although at times he also criticizes him with resources drawn from Husserl. Yet, Heidegger does not go far enough in Marion's view. Instead of turning all phenomena into objects like Husserl did, for Heidegger the language of being is paramount and all phenomena become beings (or entities, as some Heidegger scholars say in English to avoid the confusion between Being as such, beingness, and beings). Marion contends that this still does not allow phenomena to appear entirely from themselves, but restricts them to appearing as beings. Thus, both Husserl and Heidegger limit the phenomenological project in Marion's opinion, because they impose restrictions on how things are to appear, namely as objects or beings, respectively.

Marion works out this critique – at times pitting Husserl against Heidegger, at other times the reverse – in his first explicitly phenomenological work, *Reduction and Givenness*, which is a critical reading of various aspects of the two phenomenologists' work (to a lesser degree also of Derrida's reading of Husserl). In this work he argues that Husserl and Heidegger both glimpse the promise of givenness in different ways but do not work it out fully and hence remain in the thrall of metaphysics to a greater or lesser extent. Beyond the claim of the object and of being, a different call emerges: the appeal as such that would lead to a purified and more radical version of phenomenology, no longer indebted to metaphysics. This more radical version of phenomenology can be reached by exercising the phenomenological reduction more fully. Beyond a reduction to objectness (Husserl) or beingness (Heidegger), we need to operate a third reduction, a reduction to givenness. This third reduction Marion works out in much more detail in his most extensive and most systematic phenomenological work, *Being Given*. He begins by pushing Husserl's and Heidegger's basic phenomenological principles that every intuition must be received for how it gives itself and within the limits that it gives itself and the call 'back to the things themselves' to a more radical and more consistent principle that maintains that the more radically reduction is practised, the more fully givenness will emerge (BG, 10–19). That is to say, just as a liquid is chemically 'reduced' in order to get to its purest level and to identify it most fully, so operating the phenomenological reduction – setting aside anything that distracts from the experience of the phenomenon and hence overcoming any limits that would distort it or hinder it from appearing on its own terms – will allow phenomena to appear most fully and most authentically. Marion hence argues that phenomena must be liberated entirely to be given or to give themselves (*se donner* expresses both the passive and the reflexive in French) on their own terms, without any parameters imposed upon them. He asserts that such restricting parameters include their being constituted (usually as objects) by a transcendental ego, as Husserl did, or as beings experienced by Dasein in Heidegger's sense. If these horizons of constitution are set aside, then the phenomenon can appear or be given more fully from itself.

For example, Marion cites the phenomenon of a painting: it is neither appropriate to speak of it primarily as an object (especially one with a price in the market economy), nor does designating it as a 'being' really tell us much about the phenomenon; for example, when we admire the painting we are not usually all that interested in what sort of paint pigments or frame are used. The distinction Heidegger draws between things being simply present and being useful to us ('present-to-hand' and 'ready-to-hand') is also not adequate to the painting, which is not properly evaluated in terms of its existence or its utility (see also NC, 194–200, where he returns to this distinction more generally). Rather, paintings have an effect, an aura, they strike us not because of what they are but what they do to us – the effect they have on us. Marion is not arguing that the language of the object or of being is never appropriate for phenomena or that constitution in Husserl's sense might not be fitting for some phenomena. But he does point out that for many phenomena it is indeed not helpful and does not describe them accurately. Should such phenomena simply be excluded from phenomenological investigation or can we extend the scope of phenomenology to be open to all phenomena as they give themselves and in the very way they give themselves? In fact, Marion concludes, ultimately even objects can be validly examined as 'givens' and the horizon of givenness can therefore resituate all phenomena, not only very special ones (BG, 23–8).

How can this be accomplished? Marion contends that the problem is that in Husserl, intentionality plays far too large and imposing a role. Intuition is always assumed to be limited (we can never see the whole object at the same time from all sides) and falls short in presenting the phenomenon. The reduction must hence provide much of the phenomenon via intention, which Marion interprets to mean the imposing of concepts and expectations on the phenomenon. This is perfectly appropriate in the case of mathe-matical objects: we never have an intuition of a circle, but only of approximately circular objects, thus the mathematical concept of the circle is far more exact and perfectly expresses what 'circle' means – the circle is given to consciousness entirely via the concept and does not require much or any intuition. Many basic objects, especially the objects of technology, similarly provide very little intuition and concepts are imposed on them even for their 'mass' production; they are all alike, we do not need to see many of them in order to 'get' them, their particularity does not interest us in the least: one will do as well as the other. Yet, there are phenomena where this relation between intuition and intention, intuitive given and conceptual intending is reversed. Some phenomena are so rich, so overwhelming, give so much to intuition, that we cannot possibly grasp them, certainly not all at once. Here intentionality falls short: it cannot adequately account for the phenomenon that is given intuitively. Instead of giving too little intuition (like the circle), such phenomena give too much. For these phenomena, Marion contends, the language of givenness does a far better job of providing an account of their phenomenality, their – often hidden or blinding – way of appearing. There are no adequate concepts for a life-changing event, for a monumental work of art, for the depths of pain, suffering and joy, or for the encounter with another person. All these Marion calls 'saturated' phenomena.

Marion outlines several characteristics of such richer phenomena in general. Each aspect of how the phenomenon gives itself overturns or paradoxically opposes a metaphysical (often Kantian) condition of appearing. The given comes to us from 'elsewhere' or even out of nowhere, without a clearly identifiable origin. While I can explain an object in terms of its location in space and provide an account of its origin or often even how it came to be in this spot, I cannot do so for many other phenomena that arrive more unpredictably. Furthermore, instead of being determined by space, these phenomena govern the place of experience. Marion employs the category of anamorphosis from art, which is used for paintings or aspects of paintings that require the viewer of the piece to stand in a particular place or be positioned in a particular way in order to see what is hidden in the painting, which remains inaccessible except when viewed from this specific location or position. Thus, Marion concludes, the painting imposes its perspective on the viewer rather than the observer imposing the perspective on the painting: I can only see or experience it if I stand in the place the phenomenon points out to me; otherwise it remains hidden or obscure. Instead of being necessary, the given phenomenon is always contingent, sudden and surprising. It arrives on its own without prediction or anticipation. This surprising and sudden appearance also means that it cannot be repeated or controlled. Appropriating Heidegger's language of facticity – applied by him to human Dasein – Marion speaks of the facticity of the phenomenon: it comes as a *fait accompli* that is unforeseeable, uncaused and 'makes' (*fait*) itself. In many ways the given phenomenon is like an accident; its incidental nature is disturbing and disruptive, out of the ordinary and unpredictable. Indeed, the event of the phenomenon is like an effect that precedes its cause. It happens so suddenly that we do not see a cause preceding an effect, but must try to trace the effect back to a cause. The effect seems larger than the cause. The phenomenon is without measure, unrepeatable and excessive. It is simply 'given' to us and we must scramble to deal with it. It 'saturates' and overwhelms our capacity to understand or give meaning to it.

2. Saturated phenomena

Marion distinguishes between what he calls 'poor' phenomena and 'saturated' ones. Poor phenomena are those such as mathematical or technical objects, in which very little is given via intuition and much of the 'content' has to be supplied via intention. We can preview or anticipate them with ease, observe them dispassionately, understand them perfectly. Most importantly, we are generally in control of them, can impose our will on them, handle them as we wish. We are able to constitute them phenomenologically without much trouble. Saturated phenomena, in contrast, escape our grasp. They overwhelm our intuition, provide us with so much that we cannot possibly hold or understand it all. Often, we cannot bear their excess, their brilliance, their dazzling nature. They usually come to us seemingly out of nowhere, we cannot foresee or anticipate them. At times they even impose a certain control on us: saturated phenomena determine and reorient us. They are given to us, we do not control them. We simply receive them (more on that in the following chapter).

While Marion's earliest proposals of the saturated phenomenon sometimes gave the impression that it is immensely rarefied, hardly ever experienced by anyone, and possibly always endowed with a religious or mystical aura, he clarified later that such phenomena, while they might not be as frequent as objects, are experienced by anyone and to some extent are even quite mundane. Most of the saturated phenomena indeed have nothing to do with religion at all, but are manifested in everyday life. In an important essay on the 'banality' (i.e. general accessibility) of the phenomenon, he gives examples relating to the five senses (VR, 127–33). The colours red, yellow and green can be experienced as a poor phenomenon, providing only information, such as a traffic light, or as a rich phenomenon, such as a Rothko painting, that floods our sight with intense visibility. Hearing an announcement over the loudspeaker at the airport relays objective knowledge, while the voice of the opera diva is enjoyed even if I do not understand a word she is singing. The smell of gas warns me of danger, while we 'drink in' the fragrance of a perfume. Finding myself in a dark room, I try to identify the objects over which I stumble in attempting to find the light switch, while the caress with which I touch the beloved is not at all about identifying or gaining information. Poor and saturated phenomena are as different as drinking poison and tasting wine. And, so Marion claims, everyone experiences this difference. A saturated phenomenon is thus not something obscure or mysterious – at least not in the sense that we would have no clue what he means. It is simply concerned with the manifestation of phenomena that are not objects and for whom the language of objectness or signification makes little sense. They instead provide their own reason and must be analysed on their own terms.

Marion generally distinguishes between four categories of saturated phenomena, relying on Kant's descriptions of the conceptual schema that makes sense of phenomena, but overturning his categories at each point. Phenomena can be saturated in terms of *quantity*: they give too much, far more than can be grasped by intentionality. Thus, historical or cultural events can be so immense, so life-changing, so multifaceted and complex that they cannot possibly be grasped in one account (or even several). For example, we keep writing new histories of World War I or II, there are continually new interpretations of George Washington's or Abraham Lincoln's presidency, all seeking to provide an account of these phenomena and the tremendous impact they had. Or an event like 9/11 utterly and completely alters the world as we know it. Although we cannot grasp it – especially not at the moment when it occurs, when it is intuitively given – we know that nothing will ever be the same again. No categories exist for making sense of the event; we cannot mentally recreate or even fully imagine it, even via intuitive repetition such as playing the images over and over again. It gives too much. This occurs even on more personal levels, such as the event of a friendship or the occasion of a lecture (Marion examines these two phenomena as examples in the second chapter of *In Excess*) that can never be reproduced in exactly the same way. In fact, all saturated phenomena have some element of this event-like character to them. (Marion elaborates the phenomenon of the event again in greater detail in the final chapter of *Negative Certainties*, focusing especially on the fact that it cannot be predicted and is hence 'unforeseeable'; NC, 155–200.)

A phenomenon can also be saturated in terms of *quality*: it is too intense, too brilliant, too overwhelming to be seen. It dazzles and blinds us. Marion employs this category primarily for works of art, especially paintings, and calls it the idol (we have already examined it briefly in the previous chapter). Great works of art are so rich, so intense, that they can never be seen at once or fully. We are fascinated by them and must go to see them again and again. We continually discover new aspects of the painting, new layers of meaning, but never come to an end. Paintings cannot be reduced to concepts. As we have just seen, Marion claims this also of music: while the voice over the loudspeaker at a train station or airport merely gives us information and hence only the conceptual content matters, not the intuitive experience of the voice, the voice of the diva singing a famous aria in an opera is experienced as saturated (VR, 129). We are not interested in the content, often do not even understand the language in which it is sung, but we are overcome by the sensuous timbre of the voice, swept away by its beauty. The phenomenon is experienced most authentically, not when we can constitute it (all attempts at finding concepts or even words to describe it fail), but when we are submerged in it and overwhelmed by it.

A third category of saturated phenomena are those that defy the Kantian category of *relation*, namely the experiences of our flesh. (Marion relies heavily on French philosopher Michel Henry and his phenomenology of the flesh for his account.) Phenomenology early on started drawing a distinction between 'body' and 'flesh': while I can see and experience objects and other people as bodies, I experience only myself as flesh. If I touch myself, I can feel myself feeling. I have no such intimate experience of another's body; ultimately I do not really know what it feels like when I touch the other gently or violently. No one can genuinely share my pain or pleasure and similarly I do not really know or experience what the other is sensing. A particularly striking example of this is so-called 'phantom pain': when a limb is severed and hence is no longer 'there' to be observed, one still often feels pain as if coming from the missing limb itself. This pain defies the normal parameters of objects or even of 'being', considering the limb literally *is not* there and yet the pain is experienced. Experiences of pain and pleasure, joy and suffering are simply too intimate; they defy all categories, cannot be communicated in concepts. Of course, our bodies can be objectified: we can be treated merely as numbers in statistics, as bodies on the operating table, asked to 'rate' our pain on a scale from 1 to 10. Our revulsion at being treated in this way, even if it might sometimes be necessary for practical reasons, precisely shows how reductive this is and how much it disregards our more intimate experience of ourselves, of our flesh. The third category thus suspends our ability to establish relation between identifiable objects. The experience of the flesh is so intimate that no distance intervenes.

The final category of the saturated phenomenon is what Marion calls the icon or the experience of the other and is primarily an appropriation of Lévinas' phenomenology of alterity. Saturated in terms of *modality*, the other can never be reduced merely to a concept (or when this happens – for example, in slavery, in concentration camps, or in many immigration detention centres – it precisely means turning people into mere objects whose humanity no longer matters). We never understand the other fully, can only live with others precisely if they continually surprise us and do not become predictable automata. The language of 'object' or even 'being' is completely inappropriate for our experience of the other, especially if this is an experience of love. We do not experience the other as an entity, but rather as an incomprehensible and infinite alterity, as a face that cannot be seen. (We have already discussed this phenomenon of the face in the previous chapter and will return to it when discussing Marion's phenomenology of eros in the following chapter.)

Marion contends that all four of these types of saturated phenomena push our experience to the very edge of the phenomenal horizon. They give us too much, are experienced as excessive and overwhelming, as breaking all boundaries, transgressing all limits. We cannot grasp them or impose parameters upon them. There is a sense in which intentionality is reversed here in what Marion calls a 'counter-experience': instead of consciousness constituting the phenomenon and making conceptual sense of it, the phenomenon imposes its own rationality and constitutes the one experiencing it as its witness. Yet, saturated phenomena are real experiences and ones that can at least to some extent be described. Describing them requires giving an account of their impact, their effect, their overwhelming nature, their alterity, including the ways in which they invalidate the Kantian conceptual categories of phenomenality. But just as Heidegger insisted that the unveiling truth of the phenomenon is always accompanied by a covering over or veiling, which nevertheless ought to be accounted for, so what is 'unapparent', invisible or overwhelming in the saturated phenomenon is open to phenomenological description – on its own terms, as it is given or gives itself from itself.

3. The phenomenon of revelation

While the four categories of saturated phenomena just discussed have no particularly religious character – and Marion stresses this, emphasizing that his phenomenology is 'secular' in that sense, perfectly open to anyone and not restricted to religious phenomena – he does suggest that there might be a fifth category, an even higher and more paradoxical one. This fifth type of phenomenon does not merely go to the edge of the phenomenal horizon but transcends it entirely; it completely defies all our categories at once. In some sense it is a combination of the other four types, because it is saturated in all four respects at the same time: it gives too much, too intensely, too intimately and reverses the direction of the gaze. This is the phenomenon of revelation. Marion draws examples from the Scriptures, such as the account of Christ's transfiguration or resurrection, where his clothes appear brilliantly white, where the disciples are completely overwhelmed, where the course of history is altered. In *Being Given*, his analysis is fairly short, focusing primarily on the four Kantian dimensions that are being suspended and overturned in this paradoxical phenomenon (BG, 234–41).

A fuller example is provided by his analysis of the scriptural passage that recounts two disciples encountering the risen Christ on the way to Emmaus (CpV, 195–205). Marion contends that the phenomenon is fully given to them in intuition: they see and experience Christ; he is walking with them for several hours. Yet, they do not recognize him. Why not? Marion argues that although everything is given to them intuitively, they are lacking concepts or intentionality. They cannot imagine Christ's resurrection; they do not understand it; they cannot make sense of it. Christ has to provide the concepts, by laying out to them how all the law and the prophets speak of him. Again, they have an intuitive experience: their hearts burn within them. But they still do not quite get it. Not until Christ breaks the bread at Emmaus and gives it to them do they understand. And this is precisely the point when Christ disappears and becomes invisible. Faith, Marion suggests, does not 'compensate faulty intuition' (CpV, 195), but unfolds the abundant givenness of revelation. He concludes in a manner we will encounter elsewhere: 'What we lack in order to believe is quite simply one with what we lack in order to see. Faith does not compensate, either here or anywhere else, for a defect of visibility: on the contrary, it allows reception of the intelligence of the phenomenon and the strength to bear the glare of its brilliance' (CpV, 203). Thus, this 'pre-eminent saturated phenomenon' dazzles, overwhelms and blinds by overturning our categories. Our concepts fall far short of comprehending it; we cannot grasp it, but must accept it in the way in which it gives itself to us.

Marion stresses that he is not providing an apologia for a particular theological interpretation or making claims about some religious event actually having occurred (such as the resurrection of Christ), but is describing the 'mere' possibility of a phenomenon of revelation. If revelation were to occur, how could it be described phenomenologically? An 'adequate' description would be one that makes clear its own shortcomings, one that somehow bears the imprint of the excessive and overwhelming character of the religious experience. Marion justifies this distinction between 'possibility' and 'actuality' (or reality/effectivity) in an extensive footnote that is worth citing in full here because of the way in which it outlines the relation and difference between philosophy and theology:

> Phenomenology describes possibilities and never considers the phenomenon of revelation except as a possibility of phenomenality, one that it would formulate in this way: If God were to manifest himself (or had manifested himself), he would use a paradox to the second degree. Revelation (of God by himself, *theo*-logical), if it takes place, will assume the phenomenal figure of the phenomenon of revelation, of the paradox of paradoxes, of saturation to the second degree. To be sure, Revelation (as actuality) is never confounded with *r*evelation (as possible phenomenon). I will scrupulously respect this conceptual difference by its graphic translation. But phenomenology, which owes it to phenomenality to go this far, does not go beyond and should never pretend to decide the fact of Revelation, its historicity, its actuality, or its meaning. It

should not do so, not only out of concern for distinguishing the sciences and delimiting their respective regions, but first of all, because it does not have the means to do so. The fact (if there is one) of Revelation exceeds the scope of all science, including that of phenomenology. Only a theology, and on condition of constructing itself on the basis of this fact alone (Karl Barth or Hans Urs von Balthasar, no doubt more than Rudolf Bultmann or Karl Rahner), could reach it. Even if it had the desire to do so (and, of course, this would never be the case), phenomenology would not have the power to turn into theology. And one has to be completely ignorant of theology, its procedures, and its problematic not to imagine this unlikeness. (BG, 367 n.90)

Here Marion seems to maintain a fairly rigorous distinction between the two disciplines: while theology examines the historical events of Revelation as they have actually taken place, philosophy – or, more correctly, phenomenology – examines what an experience of revelation might look like, anywhere, anytime, setting aside any concern to prove whether it actually was a manifestation of the divine but paying attention only to the way in which it is experienced. Yet, although this surely does not turn phenomenology into theology, on other occasions Marion speaks somewhat differently of the relationship between the two and the ways in which they might influence each other productively.

Several of these texts are now included in the collection *The Visible and the Revealed*, but comments about the usefulness of phenomenology for theology can also be found in other works, such as *In Excess* and *Negative Certainties*. In an early (1992) essay on 'The Possible and Revelation', Marion suggests that while the conditions of manifestation are different in phenomenology and theology, the fact that both speak of revelation or manifestation is significant and can lead to productive cross-fertilization. As Revelation is primarily about manifestation, it is always already phenomenological on some level. And especially Judeo-Christian Revelation (Marion rarely speaks of other religions) already performs some of the phenomenological work necessary for givenness to appear, such as an unsettling of the independent and controlling subject or a challenging of restrictive horizons via its overwhelming manifestation (VR, 13–15). Already in this fairly early piece, Marion suggests that thinking phenomenology under the inspiration of the phenomenon of revelation challenges the transcendental I and the phenomenological horizon and ultimately opens onto givenness (VR, 16). This frees both the possibility of revelation and phenomenology itself.

In a slightly later essay (1993), Marion reverses the direction of helpfulness: not only can theology provide inspiration to phenomenology by pushing its boundaries or suggesting alternative models of manifestation, but phenomenology can provide 'relief' to theology by getting beyond the metaphysical constrictions usually imposed on it by the tradition. He reiterates the critique of metaphysics and the 'death of God' we have already seen in the previous two chapters. Phenomenology enables us to get beyond thinking of God as ground of all being or as causa sui. Instead it allows us to speak of the divine as the 'being-given par excellence' (VR, 62). Indeed Marion often calls the phenomenon of revelation 'the final possibility of phenomenology' (VR, 48) or its most extreme or highest instance (IE, 53). 'God' is the 'phenomenon par excellence' and experience of the divine the highest possibility of phenomenology (VR, 63–4). God gives kenotically: with abandon and via abandonment, just as the saturated phenomenon is given in abandon (l'abandon has the connotations of abundance, abandon and abandonment, i.e. of letting go entirely). Marion makes clear in this essay that the 'God' examined by phenomenology is still a philosophical reflection on the possibility of revelation and not a theological claim about God as such. He appeals to Pascal's distinction between the three orders to maintain the appropriate distance between philosophy and theology (VR, 64). All the same, philosophy has an obligation to think the divine: not only is reason pushed as far as it will go, but a new kind of rationality opens up (VR, 65).

In the first chapter of In Excess, Marion similarly encourages theologians to pay attention to phenomenology. It is precisely God's radical immanence, God's self-manifestation in the incarnation or in the experience of the innermost self (cf. the Latin phrase interior intimo meo conveying that God is closer to me than I am to myself), that allows a phenomenological investigation into such experience of revelation. While God's transcendence may well be excluded from phenomenology, God's immanence is not (IE, 24, 27). This does not constitute a turn of phenomenology to theology – as Janicaud claimed and censured in a famous 1991 analysis of the status of French philosophy, where he accused it of having undergone a 'theological turn' – but simply suggests that they might shed some light on each other without mutual annihilation (IE, 28). A theology of revelation must to some extent rely on phenomenology, which examines manifestation. Religious revelation may emerge as 'a particular figure of phenomenality' (IE, 29). Marion suggests that we might profitably read many biblical passages with the help of phenomenology and that phenomenology might learn from the excessive kind of revelation to which theology is committed and not take givenness as self-evident. At the end of his discussion of the event, he similarly suggests that the 'data of Revelation' must be treated as phenomena, although they may well receive different names in theology than they do in philosophy: the phenomenological event might be called a miracle in theology, theology might speak of election and promise differently than phenomenology, and it would use language of 'conversion' for the witness of the phenomenon or even take recourse to eschatology (IE, 53). Yet, phenomena of revelation are appropriate topics of investigation for phenomenology and it does more justice to them than the logical parameters drawn from other sciences or from metaphysics, on which theologians often rely.

Marion hence suggests a reorientation of philosophy of religion and its contribution to theology. Philosophy of religion (and certainly theology) should give up on abstract speculation about God, including whether God exists or not, and instead focus on the ways in which the divine is actually experienced and formulate more adequate tools for articulating such experience. How might the structures of such an experience or such experiences be described? Instead of trying to prove that a particular divine revelation has indeed taken place (because ultimately what would that prove anyway?), phenomenology is more profitably concerned with describing how religious experience in general works and what the patterns of its manifestation might be. This enables us to get at a more authentic and reliable account of such experiences and one that has broader applicability and might possibly even be used to discern between authentic and inauthentic religious experience – or at least to describe aberrant or outlier experiences. At the same time, it is obviously important to maintain Marion's insistence that such experiences cannot be understood in terms of metaphysical language – in other words, the language of subject and object, of clarity and distinctness. He insists on this even more fully by developing the idea of 'negative certainty'.

4. Negative certainties

Already when he first proposed the notion of the saturated phenomenon, Marion had stressed its unknowable and unpredictable character. As briefly summarized above, in *Being Given* he discusses various attributes of its experience: it comes all of a sudden without being expected or foreseen; it directs where we are to stand or how we are to behave in order to experience it, hence cannot be controlled; it comes as 'fait accompli', 'all done' and without our preparation or completion; it is an event that has no cause but in some sense imposes its own cause retrospectively; it is an incident, not necessary and defying normal logic and conceptuality, and so forth. In subsequent writings Marion formalizes this via the notion of 'negative certainty'. Just as an account can be given of the saturated phenomenon, as long as this account recognizes its own inadequate nature and bears the traces of the excess of the phenomenon, so there is a kind of certainty or even knowledge associated with the saturated phenomenon, albeit one quite different from the Cartesian certainty that relies on 'clear and distinct' ideas. (We see again how much of Marion's phenomenology is an overturning of Cartesian metaphysical categories and assumptions.)

The saturated phenomenon is so excessive that we can be quite certain that we can never grasp it fully or give a conceptual account of it. This certainty is 'negative': we can know most certainly that we will *not* be able to see it clearly or distinctly, that we will *not* be able to describe it in terms of quantity, quality, relation or modality, that it will transcend or overturn all those categories. There will be no doubt about this; we can be quite certain about it. This is, then, a kind of knowledge, albeit a negative one. And it does give us real information about the phenomenon, tells us something about its irreducible, unconditioned and unforeseeable character. We are, in a sense, describing its reverse or back view, except that this is not one that can ever be turned over or experienced via imagination or memory. Marion compares it to

Heisenberg's uncertainty principle, which constituted a real insight and advance in knowledge. It neither maintains that everything is utterly relative and up for grabs (as Einstein's theory of relativity is also sometimes misappropriated) nor does it point to a place where our knowledge is still insufficient, but with a little extra work will be filled in. Rather, it designates the real insight that one cannot measure both the velocity and the position of a particle at the same time, not because our instruments are not fine enough to detect it, but because it is structurally impossible: measuring the velocity changes the position, determining the position affects the velocity. The observation itself has an impact on the phenomenon and this cannot be otherwise. In the same way, Marion suggests, we cannot determine the position or character of saturated phenomena; their saturated character forbids it and we can know this for certain, it is not merely a lack of knowledge that could be filled in with more information. In the case of saturated phenomena, we *must* not impose or expect Cartesian certainty; their very phenomenality requires this of us – and that itself is a positive insight and enlargement of knowledge (NC, 205).

And this is particularly true of God. In the case of God we can be absolutely certain that we will never know all or understand completely. God far transcends all our expectations, imaginations, concepts or theories. Marion explores this in more detail in the second chapter of this book, which takes up a presentation at the fourth Villanova Religion and Postmodernism conference 'Transcendence and Beyond' (in 2003) on God as the 'impossible'. He reiterates here his fundamental claim that the notion of existence or the attempt to prove such existence is problematic in the case of God. We can neither know God nor have a concept of the divine – any such concept would be metaphysical and impose inappropriate restrictions on God who is essentially immeasurable, infinite, unconditioned, incomprehensible and not tied to space or time (NC, 53). Marion concludes in preliminary fashion that 'the impossibility of assigning a concept to God, then lies in God's very definition – which is that he admits of none' (NC, 55). Yet, this incomprehensibility and impossibility can become productive because it can actually appear phenomenologically. We experience God precisely as incomprehensible and the question of God continually reasserts its relevance; it is irreducible. God as question cannot be dismissed. Marion examines more closely this notion of impossibility. When we say that God is impossible or does the impossible, we actually mean impossible *for us* but not necessarily for God. Indeed, the Scriptures repeatedly recognize that what is impossible for us is, in fact, possible for God. Thus the distinction between possibility and impossibility as regards the divine is actually a human distinction that is a reflection of our own incapacity and conditions. God, who is eternal and infinite, experiences no such restrictions or conditionality (NC, 70).

In an earlier essay, Marion applies this reasoning to the notion of the miracle. Phenomenologically speaking, we often experience miracles – events that seem impossible and defy all concepts. When fortune turns suddenly and in utterly unpredictable fashion, we speak of a miracle. It is a genuine experience of a paradoxical event that overturns our expectations of what is possible. The miracle of revelation and the miracles Christ works are similarly distinguishable not by their suspending of certain natural laws, but rather by their sudden and unforeseeable nature. They are events that seem impossible to us, but are possible for God – like forgiveness of sin or the resurrection of Christ. The miracle is the event in which we allow our predetermined concepts to be swept away by the facts, by what has happened. Phenomenology gives us new access to the miracle: 'In freeing the possibility of the phenomenon as given, phenomenology makes possible possibility par excellence – the miracle' (CpV, 142). At the same time, an interpretation of the miracle can challenge phenomenology by suspending the phenomenological horizon and the transcendental subject. In the resurrection of Christ, the phenomenon constitutes the *I* and reveals it to itself (CpV, 146).

In *Negative Certainties*, Marion works out this overturning of possibility and impossibility with two examples. The first is my birth, which also cannot be comprehended in terms of standard (metaphysical) accounts of possibility, because it actually enables possibility itself. I experience my birth as a gift. Theology thematizes this in the notion of creation; as the creator, God opens radical and unconditioned possibility (NC, 76). Here possibility and impossibility do not submit to the principle of sufficient reason but operate their own rationality. The same is true in the story of the annunciation: the angel tells Mary that what seems impossible to us is indeed possible with God. What sort of power or possibility is affirmed here? It is not a metaphysical notion of omnipotence, but rather God's fidelity to the given promise. Fidelity hence transcends omnipotence (NC, 78). The incarnation and our redemption are evidence not of divine power to break logical boundaries, but rather of God's faithfulness and God's forgiveness.

Marion operates similar re-readings of standard definitions of the divine or other theological concepts in a couple of other essays. In one he examines Kant's refutation of the ontological argument and argues that God is always experienced as the 'unconditioned'. He suggests that Kant's own examples in the refutation don't quite work and that he disregards the difference between existence as applied to God and when used of anything else. Yet, this refutation can become productive: on the one hand, it actually shows ironically that the language of existence is inappropriate for God; on the other hand, God's excess beyond a concept actually functions positively, unlike what would be the case for objects. God *must* be beyond any idea we can form of the divine. Hence, 'Kant thus recovers in the form of an objection what St. Anselm discovered as a solution to the question of God: God is opened to the question when he surpasses the limits of the thinkable, that is to say, the metaphysical a priori which pretends to think him *as such*.'[1] God cannot be thought 'as such' because the divine is not submitted to conditions. God must be thought outside any (Kantian) conditions of experience. Marion here again uses the distinction between possibility *for us* and possibility for God. God transcends the boundary between the possible and the impossible, which is merely a human distinction. We hence must give up the idolatry of thinking God as such and instead focus on how God appears for us. It establishes the negative certainty that we could never demonstrate who God is as such and the positive insight that the event of the divine, the manifestation of God in Christ, survives the nihilism and atheism of contemporary culture. We can relate to the impossible by experiencing the excess of the gift of saturated phenomena in the mode of counter-experience, especially death, birth and the unconditioned gratuitousness of the gift.

In some ways, what Marion says here about the impossible and the unconditioned in regard to God is perfectly congruent with his analysis of the infinite in Descartes and Pascal or with his description of the icon. God's freedom from human notions of possibility and impossibility and the fact that God is not subject to conditions are similar moves to preserve divine incomprehensibility, actually heightened here via the notion of negative certainties. Yet, we can see even more fully here that this is not simply a negative claim or just a denial of any knowledge about God. Rather, it is a description of a real experience of the divine while delineating it in terms of the ways in which it overturns our normal expectations about experience and its various conditions. The notion of the saturated phenomenon and especially its application to the phenomenon of revelation, then, tries to provide an account of how God is actually experienced. Because the experience of the divine is such an overwhelming and excessive experience, its depiction is particularly difficult and must be marked by this excess in some fashion. Marion tries to do so – and at the same time to protect the ultimate incomprehensibility of the divine – by describing its phenomenality: the way it imposes itself in a counter-experience. God is not comprehended and yet is known in some way by being experienced. God comes to us and this advent, God's immanence, can be depicted phenomenologically because it is experienced by us. Yet, this experience must be received in some way, must be experienced precisely as a phenomenon by the one who is experiencing it. How does this occur? How are we able to receive the divine? What exactly does the phenomenon of revelation do to the one who has the experience? This is the question we will examine in the next chapter.

Note

1 'The Question of the Unconditioned', *Journal of Religion* 93 (1) (2013): 1–24.

4

Receiving God

Phenomenology focuses on the description of experience, and the previous chapter has outlined how Marion broadens such experience to account for any sort of given, especially particularly rich and intense experiences such as aesthetic or religious ones. But how are these experiences received? If they cannot be constituted in the traditional way, if there is no transcendental subject or ego bringing together the manifold of intuitions via some reflective synthesis, how are we to conceive of the subject that has such experiences? Like much of twentieth-century philosophy (particularly in France), Marion thinks that the modern (i.e. Cartesian) subject has served its time and does not provide an adequate account of human subjectivity. Indeed, early twentieth-century French philosophies, such as structuralism, tried to dispense with any notion of the subject altogether. Yet, the latter part of the century witnessed a more balanced retrieval of notions of the self. While few would advocate a return to the strong Cartesian ego that determines all else as lone subject in charge of all objects, some sense of the unity and continuity of the self seemed called for. Generally, this is referred to as the 'self' instead of the 'subject' in order to distinguish it from modern accounts of the subject – an important colloquium and subsequent book wondered about 'who comes after the subject'.[1] Marion's phenomenology makes a strong contribution to this debate by articulating a self to whom the phenomenon, whether saturated or poor, is given and by outlining how reception of saturation might occur. I examine this account closely in this chapter, beginning with the topic that has become perhaps most closely associated with Marion's work in the English-language discussion: that of the gift. Marion's reflections on the gift contain his earliest explicit considerations of the process of receiving and the nature of the recipient (1). From a consideration of the recipient of the gift, the chapter will move to Marion's more recent discussions of sacrifice or forgiveness and their implications for the process of receiving (2). Then we will consider the receptive self as witness or the one given over to the saturated phenomenon explicitly (3), and end with a summary of Marion's account of the self as lover and beloved (4). Throughout we will see how significant the language of reception is for Marion's thought about God.

1. Giving and receiving the gift

The gift has become one of the most debated topics in philosophy in recent years. The discussion was inspired to a large extent by Marcel Mauss' early twentieth-century anthropological study of the economic and social dimensions of gift-giving in Polynesian and other indigenous societies, such as the phenomenon of the potlatch. Other French thinkers, including Maurice Blanchot and Jacques Derrida, picked up on certain elements in Mauss' account. Derrida in particular shows how the practices of gift-giving in these societies seem to contradict the very notion of the gift. They are not at all gratuitous, but tend to involve reciprocal giving, where one gift called forth another – often a larger one that puts the recipient into debt and calls forth a new counter-gift. At the same time the abundant and lavish nature of the gift seeks to maintain its connotations of gratuity that cannot be reduced to simple economic exchange. Derrida suggests that there is a structural impossibility in the very notion of the gift: while it must always rely on notions of gratuity and 'self-less' giving, otherwise the very idea of the gift is cancelled, in practice it always involves reciprocity and debt. The gift continually reverts to economic exchange and simultaneously always defies it. The very notion of the impossible gratuity of the gift is necessary for and the foundation of any gift-giving, even as it can never actually be put into practice. Derrida hence calls the gift – and later also forgiveness, hospitality, the democracy to come, and various other phenomena – the impossible.

Marion became involved in this debate early on, already speaking of the gift briefly in *God without Being* and responding to Derrida's account with an early 'sketch' or outline of the phenomenon of the gift (VR, 80–100), which he elaborated much more fully in Part II of *Being Given*. Initially, his response consists primarily in breaking through the circular structure of reciprocity and economic exchange Mauss and Derrida had outlined for the gift, suggesting that there might be gifts that escape this structure by suspending one or several of its poles. Indeed, when reciprocity and an expectation of return or exchange are involved, the supposed 'gift' becomes submitted to economic or commercial considerations and to metaphysical causality and simply no longer is a gift. Genuine gifts might be described phenomenologically if they are of the sort that cannot be reduced to notions of causality or reciprocity. In this way they might also serve as models for givenness more generally and provide important pointers for the general phenomenology of givenness Marion is trying to elaborate in this book. Eliminating reciprocity and thus escaping a model of exchange is crucial to Marion's analysis. It will be important also for his analysis of love, inasmuch as eliminating expectations of reciprocity in love is one of the central aims of *The Erotic Phenomenon*. Furthermore, in both the case of the gift and that of love, Marion seeks to establish a kind of rationality or rigour of their respective notions that can be applied univocally to all phenomena that fall under their respective terms. Gift and love hence have important parallels and the same objectives are pursued in both accounts, as we will see more fully in the final section of this chapter.

How can the gift be thought outside metaphysical parameters, that is, outside of economic exchange, not reduced to presence or self-subsistence? It can be thought phenomenologically by paying close attention to how it shows itself and by reducing it to this self-showing, bracketing anything that might return it to full presence or reciprocity/exchange. Marion achieves this by bracketing in turn each of the poles of the gift-exchange: the giver, the recipient and the gift itself, the thing that is given. Interestingly, he begins with the recipient, who can be bracketed if he or she receives in such a way that no return or payment can be made. For example, when I make a donation to charity, the recipient is unknown and cannot return my gift. Or when a gift is given to an enemy or someone who is simply ungrateful and does not thank me for the gift, no return is made. Marion also cites the eschatological parable of the sheep and goats, in which Christ applauds and censures the two groups respectively for the gifts they did or did not make to the poor, imprisoned or marginalized without realizing that they were actually giving to Christ (BG, 92). If the recipient remains unknown or absent, no reciprocity or economic exchange can ensue.

Second, the giver of the gift could be bracketed as unknown or absent, as in the case of an anonymous gift or an inheritance where the giver has already died. The recipient then receives the gift conscious of a debt that precedes him or her and can never be relieved, because it cannot be returned to the unknown or absent giver. While the notion of permanent indebtedness here seems problematic – and is less emphasized in Marion's subsequent work on the gift – it does accomplish the goal of securing the impossibility of return or reciprocity. A third kind of bracketing concerns the gift itself, the thing that is being exchanged. It can easily be shown that the gift often involves no object at all and does not concern something that can be returned. For example, I may give my time or my love to others without giving them a concrete object. Or the thing I give may be a mere symbol, such as a ring or an insignia of power like a sceptre, which is incommensurable with the giving of love or power involved and merely represents them. Indeed, Marion suggests, the most precious gifts often involve the least tangible things – they literally give nothing while giving everything (BG, 104, 106).

Examining these cases, Marion contends, shows that phenomenological accounts of non-reciprocal giving can indeed be given, that the gift can be articulated phenomenologically. The gift has its own rigour, which is marked by 'givability' and 'acceptability', not by causality. That is to say, in order to qualify as a gift, all that is needed is for the gift to be given and to be accepted, regardless of whether an object is transferred or the giver and recipient are known or present. The giver must abandon the gift, let go of it, not expect a response or return. And from the perspective of the recipient, all that is necessary is that the gift be accepted without interpreting it as a transfer of property or refusing or mistrusting it. Marion concludes that this threefold reduction of the gift has permitted it to emerge on its own terms. Simultaneously, it reveals important structural similarities to givenness more generally. Indeed, in *Being Given*, the discussion of the gift is embedded between the first section on givenness and the third and fourth sections on the given. For our purposes, one of the most important insights of the discussion of the gift is the centrality of reception as 'acceptability' that has emerged in it. Marion will later point to this as the first step in overcoming the problems of the transcendental subject and to the position of the recipient as the gift's most significant contribution to phenomenology (BG, 251).

Marion does not actually speak very often of God as the giver of gifts and, in fact, in response to criticism implying this, explicitly denies that he is introducing a phenomenology in which all phenomena are divinely given gifts (BG, 71–4). Yet at the end of his discussion of the gift in *Being Given*, and after having reaffirmed yet again that the entire analysis of the gift is accomplished without recourse to theology or the divine, he does make some very brief suggestions about what it would mean to consider the gift theologically. A theology of revelation (as opposed to a metaphysical theology) would have to be a theology of the gift because it would not assume reciprocity or a transcendent condition (BG, 114). Marion says that he cannot explicate this claim here because it would require recourse to trinitarian theology, which is 'outside the scope of phenomenology as well as of metaphysics' (BG, 115). He provides only two pointers: first, in trinitarian theology all three 'poles' (Father, Son, Spirit) assume all three functions of giver, recipient and gift in continual self-less giving; second, self-giving and self-showing are not identical in theological giving because trinitarian gifts need not or even cannot show themselves to us entirely, although they are always given fully. One might actually read the accounts of sacrifice and forgiveness in *Negative Certainties* as ways of dealing precisely with this insufficiency of reception, especially but not only in regard to divine gifts.

2. Sacrificing and forgiving

In *Negative Certainties*, Marion returns to the gift again in two chapters and argues that it has its own rigour and rationality that can serve as an alternative to Cartesian rationality. In the earlier chapter (Chapter 3) he examines the particular rationality of the gift, playing again on the homology of 'gift' and 'giving'. He reiterates his account of the bracketing of giver, recipient and gift-object along with the conclusion that the logic of the gift escapes economy and exchange. In this case he contrasts the peculiar logic or rationality of gift and economic exchange with each other. Commerce requires equality of exchange or reciprocity, measure, causality and conditionality – it obeys the principle of identity, the principle of conditionality and the principle of sufficient reason. Hence economic exchange perfectly reproduces the Cartesian and post-Cartesian parameters for metaphysics. By contrast, the gift reduced to the logic of givenness defies all three of these principles and thus institutes its own logic and operates according to its own rationality. Givenness provides the phenomenological horizon for the gift and the gift shows how the logic of givenness operates.[2] The phenomenon of the gift undoes the logic of identity or non-contradiction by refusing any sort of reciprocity. The gift is not an exchange in which something is returned to the giver. It provides a new definition of possibility that is excessive and opens a realm of impossibility and inequality by abandoning itself entirely. The gift also undoes the logic of conditionality by being given outside of conditions: it opens unconditioned possibility and is not subject to control. It does not refer back to any cause or reason but simply gives itself from itself to be accepted by a recipient. Finally, the gift does not obey the principle of sufficient reason, but instead suspends any such rationality of sufficiency. Its abandon and abundance goes beyond what can be measured. Its phenomenality provides its own rationality: that of showing and giving itself on its own terms.

In Chapter 4 of *Negative Certainties*, Marion expands and to some extent amends his discussion of the gift into an analysis of sacrifice and forgiveness. While the earlier discussions of the gift in the 'Sketch' and *Being Given* implied that the gift might become visible phenomenologically, the analysis here argues instead that the gift becomes visible only 'negatively', namely when it is sacrificed or rejected. The phenomena of sacrifice and of forgiveness make visible the phenomenon of the gift, but they do so retrospectively. To posses a gift would annul it; its phenomenological character only emerges when the gift itself disappears. The process of givenness becomes visible 'negatively' via the phenomena of sacrifice and forgiveness (NC, 153). Marion begins with the phenomenon of sacrifice, arguing that the primary point of sacrifice is not the destruction of the gift or sacrificial object as is often thought: 'The definition of sacrifice as the destruction of a good as such not only explains nothing of sacrifice but could actually explain its opposite – the self-appropriation of autarchy' (NC, 117). Sacrifice is also not about an exchange of goods or even giving up a good to another, which is actually often more about gaining power over the other. Any analysis that assimilates sacrifice to a logic of exchange misses what is at stake in it as much as an equation of the gift with exchange.

It is true, however, that sacrifice maintains a relation with the gift. Marion argues that it actually constitutes a misunderstanding of the gift and that the gift emerges within the sacrifice. The unconditionality of the gift becomes visible in the sacrifice. The giver disappears in the giving of the gift because it is abandoned fully. In fact, the gift itself disappears in some fashion as gift if it is fully abandoned. Sacrifice relieves this aporia of the gift by making the giver and the process of givenness visible. Sacrifice returns the gift to givenness. It re-gifts the gift and reverses it toward the giver. It is not a counter-gift or the payment of a debt, but a reversal of the process of givenness. Marion calls it a 'redounding' or 'regifting' (*redondance* – usually 'redundancy') of the gift. He employs the story of Abraham's sacrifice of Isaac in order to show that the sacrifice consists in an acknowledgement of a gift previously spurned or assumed as a possession and hence not treated as a gift. Although Isaac had been given to Abraham and Sarah as a gift – the gift of the promise, the result of a miracle, the son of their old age – they had both begun to appropriate him as a possession, as their own and not God's. In offering Isaac back to God, Abraham recognizes or acknowledges him to be a gift. In Marion's view the sacrifice is fully accomplished, although Isaac is not killed, namely by Abraham's recognition of the divine gift. The gift is re-given: Isaac is given a second time and God becomes more fully visible as giver of the gift. Sacrifice, then, 'is a redounding of the gift originating with the recipient' and a bracketing that 'allows the giver's gesture to rise again to the visible' (NC, 132).

Marion's second analysis in the chapter concerns forgiveness, which even has an etymological connection with the gift (even more obvious in French: forgiveness is *le pardon*, the gift is *le don*). Forgiveness accomplishes the reverse of sacrifice. While in the sacrifice the gift was initially accepted but subsequently forgotten, in the case of forgiveness the gift was initially spurned but is then received. Instead of exceeding justice (as the sacrifice does), the case that calls for forgiveness is lacking justice; in the first case exchange is surpassed, while in the second it is never reached. The gift has been spurned, the giver rejected, the gift lost. Forgiveness allows it again to circulate, but beyond any notions of re-established justice or payment of a debt. Marion illustrates this with the figure of King Lear in Shakespeare's play of the same name, in which the king initially attempts an exchange of power for love. He spurns his youngest daughter Cordelia's gift of love, does not recognize it as a gift, and rejects her. Cordelia does not think of love in terms of the logic of exchange and Lear finally comes to realize this. Only when he asks her forgiveness in the final act of the play does Lear acknowledge the initial gift of her love. Marion claims that forgiveness is not possible without a prior gift, which it acknowledges (NC, 143). Forgiveness phenomenalizes, that is, makes visible and shows forth, the prior rejected gift. It not only enables the gift to appear, but shows its incommensurability with any logic of exchange. While in the case of sacrifice the giver re-gifts the gift, in the case of forgiveness the recipient ultimately makes the gift visible, allows for its re-gifting or redundancy. The giver and the gift are finally recognized as such, from the point of view of the recipient, in the request for forgiveness.

Interestingly enough, Marion claims at the end of his analysis here that this definition of forgiveness as the return, redounding or redundancy of the gift implies that only God can truly and fully forgive (NC, 146). What is impossible for us, namely forgiving the unforgivable, is possible for God. God forgives without limits, including any human sin. God can forgive anything because everything appears as gift to the divine logic. God continually re-gives all gifts as the very fount of goodness and giving. Marion concludes the chapter with a further illustration drawn from the Scriptures: the parable of the prodigal son. Although it is here the son, not the father, who thinks of love as an issue of exchange and misses the generosity of the other's love, the logic is the same as in *King Lear*. The son appropriates the gift of the father as a possession, as something belonging to him by right, disregarding the fact that everything the father has is his already and that his request for the inheritance is a request to possess the father's 'essence' (*ousia*). The son squanders the inheritance and finally even his filiation, envisioning himself as a servant in his father's house. In the father's forgiveness, which the son does not even expect or demand, the gift is re-given and for the first time recognized: the son was dead and is now alive. Father and Son are mutually recognized in a quasi-trinitarian sense (NC, 151). The father's exchange with the older son confirms this. This son had also thought of the father's gift as a possession and does not see the father's love for him. And again Marion points to the parallels of the father's words to the son within the parable to the words of Christ to the Father in the high-priestly prayer in John 17: You are always with me; all my things are yours. Forgiveness, then, reveals the trinitarian logic of the gift. We thus end, as in the previous section, on a theological note, albeit only with a hint of what such 'theo-logic' of the gift would mean.

More generally, the discussions of the gift, of sacrifice and of forgiveness have highlighted the centrality of receptivity. The gift must be received; sacrifice and forgiveness emerge as possibilities of reception when the original reception has failed in some way, either by being turned into possession or by being rejected entirely. Receptivity is a key notion in Marion's work and most fundamentally characterizes the self he seeks to formulate. While the metaphysical subject exercises control, self-sufficiency and autonomy, the phenomenological self that comes after the subject is the self to whom the phenomenon is given, the 'dative' of phenomenality (rather than the nominative subject as in Husserl, the genitive Dasein of Being as in Heidegger, or even the accusative 'me' as in Lévinas), it is the self that *receives* the phenomenon. Receptivity, as it has already emerged in the analysis of the gift, encapsulates everything the Cartesian subject would want to oppose: it is not in control, not self-sufficient and not autonomous.[3] Instead it receives itself from what is given to it. The self is not in a position of mastery in regard to the gift, but always its humble recipient; otherwise its gift-character is erased and it is again seen only within the logic of exchange. Marion expands this to speak of the self more generally, as the one who receives any given phenomenon. He employs a variety of figures to describe this process of receptivity: the notion of the *interloqué* (usually translated as 'interlocuted' or addressed, but meaning 'taken by surprise' or called to give account), of the witness, of the one to whom something is attributed (*attributaire*) and finally of the *adonné*.

3. Receiving the saturated phenomenon

The final part of *Being Given* analyses the new self 'after the subject' most fully. Marion employs the French term *adonné*, which is etymologically related to the titles of the other sections: givenness (*la donation*), gift (*le don*) and the given (*le donné*), hence rendered into English as 'the gifted'. More accurately, *adonné* means devoted, given over to, even addicted. This expresses exactly how Marion portrays the self that receives the phenomenon: it gives itself to it, becomes devoted to it, even addicted to it. This receptive self is always second in regard to the phenomenon; it does not anticipate or control the phenomenon, but responds to it. This has led many critics to assume that Marion's version of the self is entirely passive. Indeed, Marion critiques the kind of activity associated with the Cartesian subject, the sort of active stance that predetermines the phenomenon and only allows it to appear on the subject's terms and conditions. And the fact that he does occasionally use the language of passivity, especially in his earliest writings on this topic and the notion of counter-experience, in which the self is constituted by the phenomenon, also invites such conclusions. Yet, as we will see, the opposition between activity and passivity really misses the point of the account, which is most fundamentally about receptivity. As Marion says at one point: '*L'adonné* is therefore characterized by reception. Reception implies, indeed, passive receptivity, but also demands active capacity, because capacity, in order to increase the measure of the given and to make sure it happens, must be put to work – work of the given to receive, work on itself in order to receive' (IE, 48; see also note 7 in VR, 174 and CQ, 67–95). Let us examine more fully how this receptivity works.

Marion initially speaks of this self as a witness or as someone who has been called or 'interlocuted' – i.e. called, surprised and called to account (the French has all of those connotations). I am called by 'an inconceivable, unnameable, and unforeseeable instance which is comprehended less than it surprises and which initially remains anonymous' (RG, 199). I am claimed or convoked in the accusative, no longer the nominative subject that exerts power over objects. The self listens to the appeal of the phenomenon and responds to it. He draws on Heidegger's account of the call for inspiration here, but also relies on Lévinas' injunction to hear the call of the other. Instead of preparing for the phenomenon, laying down its conditions, defining and appropriating it as one might an object, the self finds itself called by the phenomenon, summoned to its reception. It comes suddenly, seemingly out of nowhere, without prediction or assurance, defying all traditional parameters of comprehension. The recipient is overwhelmed and, as one colloquially says, 'blown away' by it. And yet its sudden appearance requires a response. I cannot remain indifferent, but must take a stance and am called to account. Even attempting to ignore it or walk away is a reaction or response to the phenomenon (just an eminently inappropriate one). I must try to bear its impact, try to do justice to its weight, knowing full well that I cannot grasp it and cannot measure up to it, that it is more than I can bear or communicate.

The notion of counter-experience, which Marion first employs in *Being Given*, takes up this idea of being called and even constituted by a prior claim or appeal. It designates a genuine experience but one that is not a simple spectacle I could describe. Instead it is an experience of 'its own powerlessness to master the measurelessness of the intuitive given' (BG, 216). I become constituted as the witness to the event. I cannot constitute it or give full signification to it. The witness always comes after the event and is constituted by it. The self relinquishes its initiative and instead provides testimony to what has happened to it. Here Marion does use fairly passive language: the witness 'lights up as on a control panel at the very instant when and each time the information he should render phenomenal … arrives to him from a transistor by electric impulse without initiative or delay' (BG, 217–18). This is reinforced by the translation of *se donner*, which must choose between the phenomenon 'giving itself' and 'being given'. The French has both connotations, but the English translation almost always chooses the first (Marion does, after all, speak of the 'self' of the phenomenon repeatedly), which makes it seem as if the terms of the relation between subject and object are simply reversed or turned upside down, turning the phenomenon into the new subject and the receiving self into its object. Yet although Marion is indeed trying to counter strong notions of subjectivity in the transcendental subject (not only in Kant but also in Husserl), this is not simply a reversal of the terms. Marion begins his analysis in Part V of *Being Given* with a review of all the problems that emerge in traditional notions of subjectivity, such as its solipsism, its lack of individuation, its inability to distinguish clearly between a 'transcendental I' and an 'empirical me' and that very split (between *I* and *me*) within the subject itself. He proposes that the self instead receives itself from what is given to it, namely the phenomenon that arrives and demands to be phenomenalized. Indeed, Marion maintains repeatedly that the origin of the saturated phenomenon remains anonymous. It is only in the reception of the phenomenon that we can identify whether the phenomenon comes from God, from Being (cf. Heidegger), from the Other (cf. Lévinas), or from the flesh (cf. Henry). This suggests that the recipient actually plays an extremely important role of identifying the incoming phenomenon. Although this is not a Cartesian subject that determines the phenomenon, foresees, controls or even creates it, there can be no phenomenon without someone actually experiencing and identifying it. The phenomenon requires the reception by the one who phenome-nalizes it as a screen or wall hit by light first makes the light visible. The phenomenon cannot emerge (show, manifest or give itself) as a phenomenon if it is not phenomenalized, if it is not a phenomenon *to* someone. The arrival of the phenomenon must be marked by a recipient who notices it, experiences it and ultimately seeks to describe it or provide an account for it. The recipient functions as the filter or prism or screen for the phenomenon: 'Beyond activity and passivity, reception gives form to what gives itself without yet showing itself' (BG, 264). This impact of the phenomenon functions indeed like a call or appeal, especially in the case of saturated phenomena, which each issue their own kind of claim. Without making the call visible, bearing its impact like a screen makes visible the light that hits it, no phenomenon would occur or be manifested. Although the receiving self is second and does not initiate the phenomenon, the phenomenon requires the self for its self-manifestation. The call is shown in the response (BG, 282).

Marion employs Caravaggio's painting of the calling of St Matthew to illustrate this: Christ's call becomes visible only in Matthew's response, which is not spoken but expressed in his gaze directed in surprise toward Christ and acknowledging the call. Similarly, God can only speak to Samuel when he no longer thinks Eli is calling him but acknowledges himself as the servant of the Lord who addresses him (BG, 286). While the phenomenon cannot do without a self that receives it, it is the task of the recipient to listen and respond to the phenomenon, bear its impact and sensitively 'unpack' and describe what has occurred as faithfully as possible. This is indeed an undergoing, a response, a position of receptivity, not a subject in control of the objects on which it imposes its aim and thought. It is experienced as coming always belatedly and as undoing any attempt at authenticity or self-sufficiency. Yet, the recipient bears tremendous responsibility for the phenomenon: there is no phenomenality without a self undergoing the experience; the recipient is, as the final, crucial line of this part of *Being Given* stresses, 'in the end the sole master and servant of the given' (BG, 319).

The reception of the phenomenon actually requires enormous strength, which becomes visible in the many ways in which the recipient can fail to phenomenalize the phenomenon appropriately. The call of the phenomenon is delayed by having to wait for a response and that response is often inadequate. Because the call comes anonymously, I may misidentify it or fail to hear it at all. I can be blinded by its excess or experience its fullness as an absence. Instead of giving a 'sensible' account, I may be reduced to fainting, babbling, an inability to speak or even to contempt. Yet often the possible failure at the same time signals the ways in which the phenomenon and the response to it escape metaphysical parameters. Marion explores this most fully in the idea of resistance to the given. While we might think of resistance as primarily negative, as a kind of refusal, resistance to the phenomenon actually makes it visible by showing what I can bear of it. Thus my resistance is a way of holding up under the pressure of the phenomenon: '*L'adonné* phenomenalises in receiving the given, precisely because it is an obstacle to it, stops it in blocking it and fixes it in centring it. If *l'adonné* therefore reveals the given, it is in receiving it with all the vigour, even the violence, of a goalkeeper blocking a shot, of a defender marking, of a receiver sending back a winning return' (IE, 50; see also VR, 139–41). Both the phenomenon and the self are phenomenalized in this process of resistance. The greater the resistance, the more the phenomenon becomes phenomenalized.

This is especially clear in the case of the artist, where Marion speaks of it even as a kind of inventiveness. Although the artist has been 'gifted' with the sight of the unseen, he or she now bears the responsibility for transferring this phenomenon to the realm of the seen and producing a work of art that could convey the vision that has been given: 'the painter renders visible as a phenomenon what no one had ever seen before, because he or she manages, being the first to do that every time, to resist the given enough to get it to show *itself* – and then in a phenomenon accessible to all' (IE, 51). Thus, the artist is not a subject in control of its object, simply deciding arbitrarily what to create out of nowhere. Rather, the artist is inspired and gifted with a vision of the unseen, in no way in control of the artistic process. And yet the rendering of the phenomenon into visibility is an eminently active process that demands great skill, talent and finesse. Genius is simply the 'great resistance to the impact of the given revealing itself' (IE, 52). The artist is no mere object at the mercy of a new 'subject' (the phenomenon). The language of 'subject' and 'object' simply misses what is at stake in the process of artistic inspiration and creation. Even the observer or witness of the work of art, who does not initially create it but admires and responds to it, is not simply passive. We must go to see the work of art, indeed must go over and over again; we become its devotees. (Marion has elaborated his aesthetic insights even more fully in his recent book on the painter Gustave Courbet.)

In a less explicit way, this is true of all saturated phenomena and their respective recipients. All require the strength to 'bear up' under them and give some sort of account of the experience. The process of reception, although it does not involve foreseeing, controlling or dominating, is nevertheless not at all passive. It requires discipline, effort of the will, single-minded devotion, maybe even great expense of time, money and energy. And it also calls for a careful and responsible description and interpretation (what Marion calls an 'endless hermeneutics'), while knowing full well that it will fall short and that the process of providing an account of the experience may have to be repeated over and over again. This is why the response cannot be taken for granted. The phenomenon calls us to give ourselves to it, to become devoted to it, to love it, but it does not compel this love and devotion. Marion's phenomenology of love carries this analysis of givenness and its receptivity to its apex.

4. Loving and being loved

Marion's discussion of love reinforces this emphasis on receptivity, rather than simply a reversal of subject–object relationships. In *The Erotic Phenomenon*, I first insist that the other love me, then after discovering this to be impossible, I try to love myself, which also does not work. I therefore must proceed to love the other unconditionally and without any expectation of response. Yet, by the end of the work I discover myself loved by another prior to all my attempts at love and hence find myself loved after all. The topic of love is absolutely central to Marion's work and in many ways it can be said that one of the main aims of his phenomenology is to make a place for love in philosophy again. The fullest articulation of Marion's thought on love is, of course, in his book *The Erotic Phenomenon*, although he prepares this discussion in various ways in his earlier books, especially in an essay on Lévinas, 'The Intentionality of Love' in *Prolegomena to Charity* (PC, 71–101). His analysis of Augustine's *Confessions* develops some of the implications of *The Erotic Phenomenon* in a more explicitly theological vein, while *Sur la pensée passive de Descartes* does so in a more exclusively philosophical manner. I will here summarize primarily the more detailed and developed account provided in *The Erotic Phenomenon*, although I will refer back to and integrate earlier and later discussions as appropriate. Marion contends that his analysis of love has three philosophical aims: to free love from any notion of reciprocity and the logic of being; to show its own specific rationality; and to maintain its univocity in one coherent concept of love (EP, 4–6). The parallels to and continuities with his earlier work are thus apparent from the outset.

The Erotic Phenomenon posits itself as a rewriting of Descartes' *Meditations*, beginning with a sort of radical, systematic doubt that strips all assurances down to a zero point of 'hatred of all against all' and then rebuilds the experience of love from scratch via six 'erotic' meditations. Marion begins with our great desire to be loved. We are more interested in love than we are in being, thinking our lives not worth living if they include no love or affection. Without love, life seems meaningless, being no longer matters, and the question of vanity 'what's the use?' arises (as Marion had already suggested in *God without Being* and *Reduction and Givenness*). In the erotic reduction – a reduction where everything but the desire for love is bracketed – space and time have to be rethought, suddenly the 'over there' matters more than the 'here' and the expectation of the 'not yet' (or the 'no longer') more than the permanent presence of the 'now', especially if I am not loved here and now but seek such assurance from elsewhere. Furthermore, my identity becomes less about my existence than about my exposure to the other who touches me, who may or may not love me. The central question, then, is: 'Does anyone out there love me?' (EP, 40). We desperately want assurance that someone loves us and seek that assurance relentlessly from others. In this process we realize that no one can satisfy our great desire for love and hence try to love ourselves. But we cannot really love ourselves; 'loving requires distance and the crossing of distance' (EP, 46). We cannot maintain ourselves in being (as the philosophical claim of the *conatus essendi* suggests) because our being is meaningless if it includes no love. Furthermore, the attempt at self-love makes us fully aware that we are not truly worthy of such unconditional love and certainly cannot provide it for ourselves knowing our faults and inadequacies full well. From self-love we are hence led to self-hatred. We also discover that everyone else wants such limitless love and that they are similarly unworthy of receiving it. We despise them for it, despise ourselves and end up in a situation of hatred of all against all. We sink into a hole of despair where everything seems pointless and meaningless. The aporia of assurance leads to vanity and the war of all against all.

The only way to escape this experience, in Marion's view, is to give up on our own desire for love and affection, which is also rooted in the expectation of reciprocity about love: 'I will play the game of love, certainly, but I will only risk the least amount possible, and on condition that the other go first' (EP, 69). This is not love but commercial exchange. We must convert the question 'Does anyone love me?' into a different one, 'Can I love the other?' and decide to love first without expectation of response. When I decide to love first, I do not receive assurance that I am loved, but I do receive assurance of loving. This serves at the very least to individuate me as lover: 'I become myself definitively each time and for as long as I, as lover, can love first' (EP, 76). And it breaks with reciprocity: we give love instead of receiving it, love without expectation of return or reciprocity; we love entirely without conditions. This 'advance' of love has to be sustained even if there is no response to our love. As Paul stresses in his famous chapter on love in 1 Corinthians 13, to which Marion alludes here, love bears all, believes all, hopes all. In order to qualify as lover, the only thing required is decision and commitment to love, not necessarily its perfect execution. If I am fully committed to love, then I love for the sake of love. Intuition is entirely filled with love, although no clear signification can be attributed to it; it must come from the other. Consequently, the erotic phenomenon must become a 'crossed' phenomenon: the gaze of two lovers willing to expose themselves to each other, a sort of mutual vulnerability. Both expose themselves to the other, assure the other of their commitment to love via an oath or promise, yet without erasing the distance between them or fusing into a common phenomenon (EP, 105).

The mutual commitment, where each gives him- or herself to the other without requiring a reciprocal commitment but recognizing and acknowledging it in the oath, leads to an analysis of the flesh. The mere declaration of loving commitment is not yet sufficient to individualize the other, but could apply to *any* other. In my desire for the other I recognize myself and become individualized as this self, loving once and for all. Thus I come to depend on the other, I become a self in my commitment to and advance toward the other and in the risk of loving without expectation of a (reciprocal) response. This passivity or dependence does not designate a lack of activity but rather the exposure of my flesh. What I feel in my flesh opens the world for me. And I can neither feel the other's flesh as it experiences my touch nor can I feel the other's flesh inside myself, yet my flesh can expose itself, naked, to the other, not as an object but by enabling the other to phenomenalize his or her own flesh via my erotic touch. In the erotic encounter – as opposed to the encounter of objects or bodies – we enable each other to feel ourselves by offering no resistance to the other's touch, as objects would. The beloved other gives me to myself and I give the other to him- or herself. I receive the other's availability and the other receives mine and from this we each receive ourselves. In this, again, 'every static opposition between activity and passivity becomes outmoded' (EP, 122). It is a process without end or limit, where I deliver myself to the other and thereby also deliver the other to him- or herself. The continual advance and withdrawal of the flesh enables the mutual eroticization. Yet, there is a point at which it stops or is suspended; the flesh cannot maintain eros infinitely. The moment of the highest pleasure becomes erased and ends in disappointment. My finitude condemns me to repeating the eroticization of the flesh continually anew; I am unable to maintain it infinitely – which would carry me outside the world (EP, 143).

Because eroticization ceases and is ultimately always suspended, I become suspicious whether anything has actually occurred: whether I glimpsed the other's flesh but, more profoundly, whether the other actually felt anything. I do not necessarily reach the other in person; the other is not fully individuated yet. As I can deceive the other, the other can lie to me, be unfaithful to me or break my trust. Marion explores various sorts of deceptions, delusions and perversions of love, including jealousy and hatred. We can only reach the person of the other in the eroticization of the flesh if it is free, not tied to the automatic reactions of the flesh, hence only if I make love not physically but by speaking. Chastity, Marion suggests, may well be 'the erotic virtue par excellence' (EP, 183).

How is the faithfulness of love maintained that would enable the erotic phenomenon to endure? Faithfulness always has to refer to eternity; I cannot say 'I love you' honestly and mean by that only for a limited period or to a certain degree. Love always requires a complete commitment of fidelity. Faithfulness temporalizes the erotic phenomenon in past, present and future. Yet, how can I confirm the other's faithfulness? I can do so, Marion suggests, via a mutual assurance that gives the other his or her ipseity. Yet our love must continually begin again, as must its oath, its assurance, its fidelity. A third who is the result of our love might confirm this oath more permanently: the child. The child produces the oath visibly. Phenomenologically speaking, 'the passage to the child has the function of producing a more stable visibility of the erotic phenomenon already accomplished by the oath and repeated by enjoyment (*jouissance*), and thus of assuring the visibility of the lovers, as it is present and to come' (EP, 197). The child is a third party that has its own flesh and yet is also an expression of the crossing of the flesh of the lovers. The child – even the possibility of the child – manifests the promise of love even if it has already been broken. And the child does not depend on the will or decision of the lovers, but ultimately always arrives in unpredictable fashion. Yet, while the child in some sense judges and even confirms the love of the lovers for each other, this does not last: the child grows and ultimately leaves.

It erases its promise of making the lovers' oath visible. The child is not simply a sum of the parents or even a unified version, but rather its own flesh. Although the child has received the gift of life from the lovers, it does not reciprocate or compensate. Another witness to the erotic phenomenon is hence required, an eschatological witness to a love that lasts for eternity. Marion concludes that 'as lover, I must, we must, love as if the next instant decided, in the final instance, everything. To love requires loving without being able or willing to wait any longer to love perfectly, definitively, and forever. Loving demands that the first time already coincide with the last time' (EP, 211). The oath of fidelity is ultimately accomplished in the adieu: the final parting unto God (à Dieu). I finally discover myself loved before all time: 'In order for me to enter into the erotic reduction, it was necessary for another lover to have gone there before me, a lover who, from there, calls me there in silence' (EP, 215).

Marion concludes his treatment of eros by reaffirming the initial goals and presuppositions; the erotic reduction has shown love to operate its own rigour and logic, which unifies love in a univocal concept but is not submitted to metaphysical parameters. This univocity of love implies for him that all love is ultimately the same; there is no distinction between *eros* and *agape*. *The Erotic Phenomenon* hardly speaks of God at all. Yet, Marion concludes that all love has to be said in just one way, and that hence God's love is identical to human love. These are not two different kinds of love, but merely variations on the same theme. We love as God loves, God loves as we love. In the final lines of the book Marion returns to this claim explicitly: 'God practices the logic of the erotic reduction as we do, with us, according to the same rite and following the same rhythm as us, to the point where we can even ask ourselves if we do not learn it from him, and no one else. God loves in the same way as we do' (EP, 222). He concludes that not only does God love exactly as we do, but is also the first lover who precedes us and loves us infinitely more than we are capable of love (EP, 222). God's love is not qualitatively different, it is just better, stronger and more persistent than ours. This is a somewhat surprising claim considering how much time Marion spends arguing against *any* univocal naming in his seminal book on Descartes' 'white' theology. Yet, love is explicitly excluded from this censure of univocity as blasphemous and Marion consistently stresses and argues for its univocal character. The main reason for this is his desire to overcome Anders Nygren's famous distinction between *eros* and *agape*, which Marion judges fundamentally false and wrong-headed (RC, 190; see also SP, 272–3). If we could not love like God then the very core of the Christian vision of redemption would simply evaporate, in Marion's view.

Why is univocity not a danger in the case of love? The main reason lies in its particular character. Love, for Marion, is always completely self-giving, utterly sacrificial, devoted to the other without hesitation or restriction. Love, as he insists repeatedly, is like a declaration of war: total, absolute and without any conditions whatsoever. The best name for this love is maybe neither *eros* nor *agape*, but *kenosis*: complete self-surrender on behalf of the other. Already in *God without Being*, Marion argues that love is not restrictive in the way in which being is, because love gives itself away and hence is not strictly speaking a 'definition' at all (GWB, 48, 107, 136–8). Love is pure, unmitigated gift. While being closes in on itself, becomes a possession and a property (as we have seen, *ousia* in the parable of the prodigal son is used for the father's inheritance requested by the son), love opens out, gives itself freely and abundantly, abandons itself to the other. It cannot be restrictive, so, Marion contends, precisely because it does not hold onto anything, gives everything freely. God is best 'defined' by this activity of self-emptying loving rather than by a static attribute or property.

The statement that God is love, made so explicitly in the Scriptures (especially 1 John 4.16), Marion suggests, has actually been for the most part forgotten by the tradition, especially by philosophy. Metaphysics cannot envision love as a definition of God because it seems far too subjective and has no capacity for attaining the absolute (CpV, 168). Yet, even theological or religious thought rarely seems to reflect on love. Marion thinks that this name for God is marginal to Islam or Judaism and ultimately only emerges in light of the cross and the resurrection. The scandal or folly of speaking about God in terms of love is that the human also can be defined primarily in terms of love. God must be understood in terms of love, but that means that God understands and practises love (CpV, 170). And Marion stresses again that this means that God loves like us, just infinitely better, in a divine fashion. God transcends us as the best lover and hence love can become a name for divine transcendence. And the infinite transcendence of God's love is measured by the depth of kenosis: by the risk God takes in loving to the point of death on the cross. God loves what is not loveable (us) without expecting a return and by risking all. And just as Christ's love for us makes visible the invisibility of the Father, so our love for each other makes visible our invisible love for God (CpV, 173). Any claim about God's transcendence, for Marion, ultimately comes down to charity and while we are called to the same love, it also infinitely transcends our capacities and must be put to work in us via Christ in trinitarian fashion (CpV, 175).

Thus, this univocity of love goes beyond even what Marion explicitly indicates: not only is divine and human love univocal, but love ultimately turns out to be univocal with the gift. Loving is identical with self-giving. The same kenotic self-abandon characterizes both moves. And this is true not only of giving but also of receiving. Receiving God, like receiving the saturated phenomenon, is ultimately about the capacity to love, a capacity for devotion and self-abandon to the other. Love, gift, sacrifice and receptivity (or even forgiveness) are in some way versions of each other. As sacrifice acknowledges the abandon of the giver's gift of love and seeks to return it, so forgiveness extends and doubles the initial unacknowledged gift of love in a renewed gift of loving abandon. 'Proper' receptivity is precisely the return of complete devotion and self-givenness to the gift of love received. We ultimately receive God in terms of love: by loving devotion to the wholly other, expecting nothing in return, dedicating ourselves entirely, becoming devoted and addicted. To receive God means to respond in loving self-abandonment to the kenotic gift of divine love. In the following chapter we will explore the more explicitly theological descriptions of this: the response to God in worship and adoration through prayer and the sacraments.

Notes

1 Eduardo Cadava, Peter Connors and Jean-Luc Nancy (eds), *Who Comes After the Subject?* (New York: Routledge, 1991). Marion's discussion of the 'interlocuted' first appeared as a contribution to this colloquium and collection.

2 Both here and in *Being Given* Marion – somewhat problematically – focuses on the notion of paternity or the gift of the Father as the

central example for such selfless giving. While in these two instances a human father seems to be meant (Marion is fairly adamant that a mother would not work as an example), in other places the Father stands for God and indeed God is almost always envisioned as Father in Marion's work. It would go beyond the purposes of an introduction to Marion's work to provide extensive critique of this, but at some point such critique appears called for.

3 One should point out, however, that not all of Descartes' talk about the self advocates a Cartesian subject in Marion's view. In an important article Marion explores a change in terminology from the Latin *capax* or *capacitas*, which designated a receptive capacity for the divine, to the much more active French *capacité*, which came to mean a human power of comprehending God or even proving God's existence. In Marion's view, Descartes' work shows this transition, although he himself does not operate it fully and hence remains to some extent in the position of receptivity *vis-à-vis* the divine (CQ, 67–95).

5

Worshipping God

Marion's phenomenology provides a framework for articulating the structures of religious experience. Such experience, in his view, is overwhelming, intense, ungraspable. That is so because God is infinite and incomprehensible. The divine cannot be expressed or articulated in metaphysical or conceptual language. How, then, can we approach the divine? We do so primarily in a position of receptivity where we are open to how the divine gives itself on its own terms. We must bear up under the divine disclosure. We must be entirely devoted in love. Yet, how does this concretely happen? Can we get beyond general phenomenological claims about the category of religious experience per se and depict concrete encounters with the divine? What might be examples of 'phenomena of revelation'?

Marion does actually write quite frequently in a more theological mode, especially in some of his early articles for the Roman Catholic theological journal *Communio*, which he helped found and with which he has been heavily involved for most of its existence, but also more recently for various colloquia or conferences. The sacrament of the Eucharist is a particularly prominent topic to which he has devoted multiple articles, but he also considers questions of faith more generally (1), describes movements of prayer (2), considers the role of the baptized Christian in the life of the church (3), and repeatedly returns to the sacraments as instances of divine gifts (4). One may well say that the various reflection on these religious and ecclesial activities serve to illustrate and apply the more theoretical structures we have examined in previous chapters: the task of faith is to explicate the alternate rationality outlined in Descartes and

Pascal, prayer approaches the divine before the icon in a crossing of gazes, the baptized Christian experiences the phenomenon of revelation, which reaches its height in the invisibility of holiness, and the sacrament in general and that of the Eucharist in particular show how we can receive the supreme gift of divine love.

1. Faith: Rationality of charity

Perhaps the most important thing that ought to be said about Marion's view of faith is that it is not opposed to reason, as is often supposed. In fact, he argues repeatedly that just as scientific investigation requires a measure of belief and assumption of certain presuppositions, so faith requires and displays rationality. In an address first delivered at the request of the late Cardinal Jean-Marie Lustiger as a Lenten lecture at the cathedral of Notre Dame de Paris (February 2005) Marion specifically confronts this question under the title 'Faith and Reason' (VR, 145–54; CpV, 17–29). He argues that believing requires giving an account (an *apologia*) of one's faith, pointing out that several prominent early Christians were also philosophers, such as Justin Martyr – in whose case 'giving an account' or providing a witness actually ultimately meant to give his life. Because Christ is the Logos, the Word or Reason of God, Christians – who, after all, bear his name – must also practise logos; they have a duty to rationality. The rationality of faith is not identical to the rationality of science, but is a different, higher kind of reason. It is a rationality of love that unfolds the reasons of love. Marion appeals here, as in many articles on similar topics, to Pascal's third order. The order of charity has its own logic and rationality, namely that of love (*caritas*), and this rationality unique to faith is inaccessible to metaphysical or more generally scientific knowledge. Marion also points out that the term 'theology' was not originally used to designate Christian accounts of faith because the term was associated with pagan religion. And yet early Christian thinkers certainly attempted to set forth the particular rationality of their religion and to defend it to others, whether to argue against persecution or to show the coherence of the new religion after the Constantinian transition. To reason about faith is not optional for Christians, but that does not mean that they must simply adopt the rationality available from other realms of knowledge – quite the contrary. Marion also points to the tremendous influence Christianity has had throughout its history on the arts and sciences and various cultural developments and achievements, many of them immensely fruitful.

What does a rationality of faith or love mean? It obviously does not involve reducing faith or God to manageable concepts over which we could be in full control. Nor does it mean approaching faith like an object over which I would be the subject wielding power. Instead the rationality of faith opens us to the realm of saturated phenomena and ultimately concerns anyone 'for whom the humanity of humans, the naturalness of nature, the justice of the polis, and the truth of knowledge remain absolute requirements' (VR, 150). The 'higher reason' of faith prevents us from the kind of scientific and technological mode of knowing that reduces everything to numbers, data, reproducible and replaceable objects. Instead it enables us to remain open to the irreducible, the irreplaceable, the unconditioned. It is thus a rationality that unfolds an experience. Faith is the response to contemporary nihilism, which, for Marion, following Nietzsche, equates with the 'devaluation of all values' by turning them into objects or metaphysical concepts, where we become, as Descartes said, 'masters and possessors of nature'. Nihilism ends in vanity, in the resigned conviction that nothing has value, nothing matters, everything is useless and meaningless. Humans are dehumanized, nature is exploited, society becomes unjust, the media distorts truth into mere information. The rationality of faith means to oppose this sort of nihilism and its detrimental effects. Christians have a genuine contribution to offer by communicating the kind of love that gives access to the logic of charity and hence opens new possibilities beyond the impasse of nihilism, consumerism and techno-science. We need a reason that does not master objects (a rationality of certainty), but instead loves the other (a rationality of charity).

Marion argues for a Christian contribution to rationality, interpreted in terms of a logic of love, in other places as well. In an essay included only in the English translation of *Prolegomena to Charity*, he contends that while Christians often speak about faith and increasingly today about hope, they pay far less attention to charity. Faith is what the past gives us of Revelation, hope anticipates Revelation's future, but love concerns its present reality. Marion equates 'present' here not only with the tense but also with gift: 'Charity renders the gift present, presents the present as a gift. It makes a gift to the present and a gift of the present in the present' (PC, 154). We see here again the equation of love with gift in Marion's work. Charity is *the* Christian requirement, yet it is not only a passion (exemplified supremely by the flesh) but also a kind of knowledge. Love allows us to know the other, not as an object but as a flesh; indeed, it is the only way genuinely to know the other or to allow the other to appear. Through love I 'set the stage' for the other and allow the other to be manifested 'as the uncontrollable, the unforeseeable, and the foreign stranger who will affect me, provoke me, and – possibly – love me' (PC, 167). This is parallel to what Marion later says in *The Erotic Phenomenon*, but here it is particularly obvious that such love is only possible through a kenotic self-emptying in which I make room for the other. Theology, Marion suggests, ought to pursue the knowledge of charity, because that is the best contribution that Christians could make 'to the rationality of the world', inasmuch as it manifests the revelation that they have received from Christ (PC, 169). The task of theology, then, is to unfold the particular rationality of Christian faith which displays the logic of charity.

The very task of apologetics, if we still want to use that term, is to lead people to love and to show people the love of God. Marion says that 'the point of apologetics is thus to lead, by the constraints of reasons, to this place, where, finally, the "heart," faced with the possible evidence of truths, passes across evidence to Love' (PC, 62). Instead of arguing people into the faith by convincing them of objectively valid reasons for belief, we are to demonstrate the evidence of love that would call forth the heart's assent in trust. To believe means to love, to have the will to believe in love: 'Nothing separates, perhaps, he who believes from he who does not believe, except this: not reasons, of course, not some certainty … but merely believing despite the belief that one does not believe. To believe in Love, and that Love loves me in spite of my belief that "I don't have faith".' It is only faith in love, then, that makes one a believer: 'Nothing separates the believer from the unbeliever, except faith, which plays out over nothing: *nothing*, which is here a way to say the oscillation of the will in front of Love' (PC, 64). Again, love and gift are equated, here by being identified with faith; to love and to believe mean to let go of one's autonomy and to surrender to the gift, to abandon oneself to the other instead of insisting on possession (PC, 64). In order to believe we simply must love. Love itself becomes an expression of faith. Faith requires a conversion of the gaze to love. And love provides evidence through the overwhelming bedazzlement provoked by revelation – that is to say, by love. A renewed apologetics can draw on phenomenology in order to make room for conversion through a defence of love. God is 'demonstrated' by being open to the revelation of the divine Love. Or, as Marion says in a different context: 'faith is the mode of knowledge appropriate to the saturated phenomena characteristic of Revelation' (CpV, 100).

Already in *God without Being* Marion had suggested that faith is not primarily a discourse but rather an activity: the activity of believing and of loving. Faith 'must be absorbed in charity' because charity is the very logic of faith (GWB, 183). Without love, theology remains mere 'scientificity'. Faith is validated not by scientific rationality but by the confession of love. Faith is primarily a decision and a commitment, but that does not imply that it is irrational or that rationality is simply bypassed or neglected. Rather, faith is the kind of performance evidenced also by performative speech that makes something happen within the act of speech (such as declaring a couple married or a building open). But who is able to perform the statement that 'Jesus is Lord' except maybe Christ himself? Charity has a rigour and a logic that is a logic of kenosis and hence requires the risk of confession instead of providing a foolproof assurance or validation. Faith cannot be based on certainty or be grounded in some foundationalist logic. Rather the confession of faith requires self-giving love and is finally 'validated' in martyrdom. Martyrdom allows the believer to imitate Christ by sharing in his passion and abandoning oneself fully to him (GWB, 197). It is, then, the ultimate validation of faith by the logic of love. God's utter self-emptying in love, the divine kenosis, calls forth a corresponding self-abandonment in loving faith from the human recipient.

Marion pursues this argument about an alternative rationality of faith even more fully in almost all the pieces included in the collection *Le croire pour le voir* – even the title suggests that one must believe *in order to* be able to see, that believing is a type of seeing (turning upside down the adage that 'seeing is believing').

Again he argues that Christian thought must resist the nihilism of contemporary culture and instead pursue an alternative model of reason. Faith requires argument, namely the argument of the passion of Christ, the reason shown on the cross. This is the dual logic of witness or testimony: rationality confirmed by martyrdom. A rational discussion does not require putting one's faith in parentheses and pretending to be able to speak from a completely neutral position, already subject to a particular (scientific) model of rationality. Marion opposes to today's 'communicational' model of reason a witness of faith that can contribute to the common good by unfolding the logic of Revelation. The 'apologetic work' of Christians is to work in the rational service of Revelation, which affirms reason against the nihilism that seeks to dispense with it and receives the divine Word. This is really the only way in which the so-called 'Catholic intellectual' (Marion does not like the phrase because in his view it smacks of elitism and militancy) might serve and love the church today, namely as part of the community of the baptized seeking to work out the rationality of their baptism and the kerygma of faith that motivates it. Such argument would consist in unfolding the truth of Revelation, the truth of the Gospel, and allowing it to affect public debate.

We hence see Marion's insights about rationality, first put forth in his work on Descartes and Pascal, which we examined in the first chapter, applied to Christian faith. Faith is not opposed to reason but operates a particular kind of reason, namely the logic of charity, the rationality of love. This reason does not provide concepts for the divine or apply metaphysical parameters to Christian faith, but instead it unfolds the logic that is already within it and that is revealed in Christ. It is a reason that moves the will and compels the evidence of love rather than a knowledge of certainty dependent on 'clear and distinct' ideas. It helps us to know, that is to encounter, the other rather than to comprehend him or her. And instead of proving God's existence, it commits to God in faith by responding to the divine love. It hence no longer speaks about God but to God. Any 'apologetic' speaking about God is actually an action: helping the other see the manifestation of the divine love and inviting the other to conversion. This is the task of faith, just as it is the task of a non-metaphysical philosophy or a phenomenology of givenness.

2. Prayer: Crossing of gazes

Marion speaks about prayer on several occasions. Already in the discussion surrounding the appropriate way to name the divine, prayer emerges as a higher way that speaks to God instead of merely speaking about God. Prayer, for Marion, consists primarily in praise. In prayer I invoke the other but without attempting to define, describe or depict. Praise raises us toward God without an attempt at controlling or defining God. It names God, but only in the form of address, not in the form of definition. Prayer is not about attributing, but about 'aiming in the direction of' or 'comporting oneself toward' or 'invoking the unattainable' (IE, 145). Prayer reverses the direction. We do not name God, but God names or calls us: 'For the Name no longer functions by inscribing God within the theoretical horizon of our predication but rather by inscribing us, according to a radically new praxis, in the very horizon of God' (IE, 157) supremely accomplished in baptism. 'This pragmatic theology is deployed, in fact, under the figure of the liturgy (which begins with baptism), where it is never a matter of speaking *of* God, but always of speaking *to* God in the words of the Word' (IE, 157). Here Marion seems to focus primarily on personal prayer, although he hints at a larger liturgical dimension: 'Concerning God, this shift from the theoretical use of language to its pragmatic use is achieved in the finally liturgical function of all theo-logical discourse' (IE, 157). What might it mean for theology to have a 'liturgical function'? At the very least it implies that engaging in theology must lead us to worshipping God, must direct us toward God, rather than merely speculating about God. Marion focuses primarily on the personal dimensions of such discourse, but occasionally also points to broader communal dimensions.

Marion does not define the content of this prayer, but instead describes more its phenomenological impact: it exposes us to the divine gaze, it gives us a name, it reorients us. Marion's discussions of prayer are closely linked to his explication of the icon, which we have already examined in detail in the second chapter. Prayer before an icon is an exposure to the divine that opens itself to the gaze coming across the icon and participates in a crossing of gazes: 'In the icon, the gaze walks along itself toward an invisible gaze that envisages it from glory' (CV, 78). The icon does not claim holiness for itself but instead returns or renders the prayer to the invisible. In venerating an icon, that is, praying before an icon, one is exposed to Christ's gaze rather than looking at it directly. If the gaze 'contemplates' God, it does not do so through a determinate vision of the divine that could figure out who God is or knows the divine nature; rather it contemplates as one admires a painting or listens to a symphony, not by analysing but by being absorbed and lost in admiration. This is why liturgy has to be performed over and over again. One prayer is not sufficient, but we must pray together again and again; perhaps we must learn to turn our entire lives into prayer. Prayer, then, is more an expression of devotion and love than it is an activity of speech. It desires to have an effect and is open to being affected. It crosses the distance to the divine without erasing this distance. It exposes itself to the other who may turn everything upside down and send me off on a strange mission.

Both accounts of prayer (about the language of praise in *In Excess* and about the crossing of gazes in prayer before an icon in *The Crossing of the Visible*) have profound parallels with Marion's discussions of love. He argues that the speech of love is like that of apophasis. In both cases, language is not concerned with depiction or predication but rather with having an effect, with getting the other to respond in a certain way. He compares Clélia's declaration of love to Fabrice in Stendhal's famous novel *The Charterhouse of Parma* to Christ's thrice-repeated question to Peter after the resurrection whether he loves him. The perlocutionary speech of love parallels the pragmatic use of language by mystical theology. Marion suggests that philosophy's suspicion of theology corresponds to its exclusion of love from rigorous philosophical engagement (VR, 116). Peter affirms his love three times, moving through kataphasis (affirmation that he loves Christ) to apophasis (undoing his twofold denial) to eminence, namely speech that has an effect ('tend my sheep'). Although Marion does not explicitly invoke prayer in this context, the parallel between erotic speech and the threefold path of mystical theology suggests that prayer is like perlocutionary speech: meant not to describe or deny, but rather to have an effect, evoke an encounter, enable a response.

An even stronger parallel is evident when Marion describes both prayer across the icon and the erotic encounter as a 'crossing of gazes'. To love is to expose myself to an invisible gaze; I do not 'fix' my gaze on the other, but instead 'face up' to the other's gaze (PC,

81). Only this self-disclosure individuates both me and the other. Love, then can be defined phenomenologically, as 'two definitively invisible gazes [that] cross one another, and thus together trace a cross that is invisible to every gaze other than theirs alone' (PC, 87). Loving is not about being seen or about desire but about 'experiencing the crossing of gazes' (PC, 87). The invisible gaze of the other weighs on mine and makes possible my own experience. And 'to support a gaze means to support the invisible unsubstitutable within it' (PC, 99). I allow myself to be summoned by the other's gaze, expose myself to the other and hence receive myself from the other. All this is said in this particular context of love, but it parallels precisely what Marion previously says of prayer before the icon, which functions in exactly the same way: I am summoned by the gaze of another, expose myself to and receive myself from the other. Prayer is a movement of love and operates according to the erotic reduction. And Marion does actually make it explicit in some cases: 'The icon has as its only interest the crossing of gazes – thus, strictly speaking, love' (CV, 87). The fact that his language about the icon shifts from his earlier considerations of religious icons or icons as a way of encountering the divine to the phenomenological category of icon as encounter with the face of the other that finds its height in the erotic encounter further cements this parallel.

These accounts and their parallels to love are also confirmed in a different mode by Marion's study of Augustine's *Confessions*, where he takes up again the topic of praise – in this case in the mode of confession. He argues that this text should not be read as an autobiography, as often happens, but rather as an extended confession, which has two modes: confession of sin (hence speaking about, or rather to, the human) and confession of praise (hence speaking about, or rather to, the divine). Augustine has three audiences: the self, God and the community of other humans. His goal is not only to praise God but to lead himself and those others who read him to praise of God. Confession is put into operation by praise; praise is its proper starting point, and the *Confessions* as a text are only understood in the mode of praise, by someone willing to praise (SP, 13–14). Marion points out that often Augustine's praise of God is actually citation: he speaks with the words of the psalmists or other biblical texts. Praise is then already a response to a call received previously. This is thus not only about the mode of writing of a particular text, but is actually a description of Christian faith: the Christian is one who exists in the mode of confession – both of sin and of praise. Before God we 'cannot not confess' and the twofold modes in which we do so, confessing our sins and praising God, are actually a mutual condition of each other: 'I can praise God only if I discover myself already a beneficiary of his mercy, therefore only if I acknowledge myself first a sinner against him' (SP, 30). Praise and confession hence express the place and condition of the self before God. And while this confession is at first individual, it ultimately becomes communal and liturgical. The text invites others to praise and lifts up our communal praise, as we discover ourselves in the place of the self. This means that we must see others in God and God in others. The other is ultimately accessible only from God's point of view: 'The other becomes visible, even for me, in the light projected upon him or her by the gaze of God and not my own' (SP, 50). Marion argues that in this way Augustine anticipates the contemporary phenomenological considerations of how to provide an account of our experience of other humans.

The book as a whole pursues many other topics (such as truth for which he again establishes a link to love and the third order of charity, the movement of the will which turns out to obey an erotic reduction, the time of advent that enables conversion, the highest name of God, etc.) in the *Confessions*, correlating them to a phenomenology of givenness and hence showing that it is not a metaphysical text, but for our purposes here I will only point to a couple more references to prayer in these later chapters. Marion shows that the self is not predetermined in Augustine, but indeed does not know itself and hence displays the characteristics of the *adonné*, the one given over to or devoted to the call that precedes it. This discovery is made within a liturgical context: 'I do indeed differ from myself, to the point of losing all knowledge of *myself*, not only in the experience of my failings (erotic desire, weakness of will) but even in the experience of my highest exaltations (in this case communion in liturgical prayer) ... Even when it prays, the ego differs from its *myself*, or rather self-differs and is therefore not appropriated to any *myself*' (SP, 66). Indeed, music enables us to enter 'into the prayers of the community of believers' in the context of the liturgical mysteries, although the emotion can also carry me away in inappropriate ways (SP, 66). The liturgical context emerges again more fully in the latter chapters of the *Confessions* that are reflections on the Scriptures as they are employed within worship in the community. This is especially true of Genesis: 'The community of believers, of those who confess God in faith, is therefore the sole thing that permits seeing and saying things as created ... because it alone hears and sees in them the goodness of God' (SP, 235). There is hence a liturgical condition for recognizing creation: theologically speaking, creation does not precede praise but indeed liturgical praise precedes creation. Thus, while the focus of the book as a whole always remains on the place of the self (as the title indicates), at moments a larger liturgical community of prayer emerges.

What might all this say about prayer? While it begins in personal, solitary prayer, it ultimately culminates in liturgy, although the reverse is also true: one begins in liturgy (via baptism) which then enables personal prayer. Within the liturgy Christ becomes present: 'Christ speaks in the readings, makes himself seen, touched, eaten, and breathed in his eucharistic body. Every liturgy effects the appearance of Christ and results from it' (CV, 64). One can certainly miss this and experience liturgy only as an idolatrous spectacle, but that depends entirely on my gaze. If I am willing to expose myself to the invisible gaze that meets me in the visible liturgy, then I become open to the splendour of the liturgy, which is the splendour of love. Prayer means to open myself to the loving gaze of the divine other and thus to the meeting of the invisible within the liturgy (CV, 65). Speaking about God is then always rooted in worship, in the liturgical life of the church, in the activity of speaking to God and being open to the divine address. The liturgical life of the church provides the context in which I can hear the divine word, become open to the divine manifestation and learn to pursue the Christian life.

3. Sanctity: Phenomenon of the invisible

Genuine worship of God extends to all of life and is not limited to the church building or even personal prayer. We are to worship God with our bodies, hearts and minds, with all of who we are. In this sense, we are to become saints. Holiness is the ultimate goal of the Christian life, if we are genuinely to become like God. Marion explores what it means to be a saint in the final chapter of *Le croire pour le voir*. He argues that the saint must by definition remain invisible, because no one can claim sanctity and because it is not governed by visibly identifiable characteristics. Just as only a great artist is a true judge of great art, so sanctity would have to be established by other saints, yet who could claim such a title? One would have to have a concept of sanctity and various exemplars of it. But just as one could not claim sanctity for oneself, one also could not really judge it in another. Holiness for Marion is closely connected with death – the witnesses to both are equally invisible and impossible. He mentions the examples of survivors of the camps: although they try to bear witness to its death machinery, really only someone who had experienced it fully, and hence would have died in it, could bear genuine witness, which is precisely no longer possible if one has died. Only someone who has returned from the dead could bear witness to it. Thus, we only have one genuine witness: Christ. Marion argues that this goes beyond mere analogy; sanctity or holiness designates what is set apart, what belongs to God and is unique and particular to the divine. We cannot even see this holiness; it is far too much to bear. It becomes visible only in the darkness of the passion or the 'semi-clarity' of the sacrament (CpV, 214). Marion refers again to Pascal's distinction between the three orders, arguing that the saints are only visible from the point of view of the third order and remain invisible to the others. Holiness or sanctity hence has its own realm of phenomenality, experienced only by those who are holy.

Indeed, despite the claim that holiness remains ultimately invisible and can be appropriately attributed only to God, Marion also understands it as a more general call for the Christian life. We have already seen in Chapter 2 that Marion calls us to become icons of God and that icons are to make visible God's invisible holiness (CV, 66). The saint is then not some special or superlative Christian, but holiness is the call addressed to every baptized Christian and constitutes the 'dignity' of all the baptized. Marion tries to recover this dignity or priesthood of all the baptized against the more recent distinction between clerics and laity. The people of God are those who are called by Christ: answering to his call and bearing his name. This name is acquired through baptism; to be a Christian is to be baptized. Marion condemns the militancy expressed in the notion of the laity and the ways in which it

becomes subject to an ideological doubling and supports a kind
of clericalism. The terminology of laity according to him seems to
assume and indeed functions as belonging to a special organization
that focuses on a particular social milieu and is called to concrete
militant actions. This kind of mobilization remains closed to the
majority of the baptized; it constitutes an elite group of activists.
These are treated like professionals who undertake Christian
conquest in terms of evangelization, which ultimately paints an
alternative salvation history and institutes a kind of social clique
that has its own ideology. Furthermore, it separates the laity artifi-
cially from the clerics who come to depend on them for their own
self-justification. All this is an ideology that in Marion's view misses
the point of the logic of the cross and the reality of revelation.

Instead of a 'promotion of the laity' Marion suggests that we
need to acknowledge and restore instead the 'eminent dignity' of
the 'poor baptized' by affirming the priesthood (*le sacerdoce*) of
both the baptized and the priests (CpV, 88). The priesthood of the
baptized is grounded in Christ and requires no further 'promotion'.
The priesthood of the priests is simply the service on behalf and
for the baptized that makes their baptismal priesthood possible
through offering the sacraments (especially baptism and Eucharist).
Via baptism and Eucharist all believers are incorporated into Christ
and thus constitute the body of Christ. The goal of the baptized
community is conversion: converting oneself and the world into
Christ: 'conversion of everything – in me, in us and in the world
– to the Father, in the Son, by the Spirit' (CpV, 90). The dignity of
the baptized, their priesthood, consists in making Christ present.
The task of the ordained priest who acts supremely *in persona
Christi* is solely to make this possible and to enable the community
to achieve this goal. The bishop or the hierarchy hence do not have
higher dignity than the community of believers: baptism confers the
highest dignity possible, namely that of faith and access to eternal
life via the conversion of all into the Word. 'What has not been
assumed, has not been redeemed' – the baptized assume Christ and
redeem themselves and the world by converting all to Christ (CpV,
95; Marion is citing a popular Patristic principle originally articulated by Gregory Nazianzen).

Marion argues that the future of Catholicism does not consist
in focusing obsessively on certain social issues or advocating for
particular engagements of social justice, but rather in becoming

faithful believers. How does such conversion happen? It is slow and risky: Marion says in the dialogue with Dan Arbib that he is 'trying' to become Catholic: 'I say that I am trying, because I make efforts, I apply myself to it, I hope to progress, but slowly' (RC, 285). Such efforts and progress consist in putting charity to work and hence to call also for the conversion of the neighbour. Indeed, in these conversations Marion shows himself quite optimistic about the future of Catholicism in France, pointing out that in comparison to many other historical periods, Christianity is doing quite well. While he acknowledges a certain demise of new vocations to the priesthood, he argues that this is a wider problem: it is true of all professions that are vocations – teaching, nursing, and so forth, all suffer from young people willing to engage in them (RC, 283). And, he points out, there are still far more priests in France than there were before the Reformation and they are considerably more committed than has been the case at many other points in Christian history. He also reminds his listeners and readers of the fact that the churches in Paris are generally full on Saturday nights or Sunday mornings and do not suffer from attendance at mass (RC, 283). While the media and popular culture may proclaim a demise of adherence to religion, this is often overstated. And finally, faith was never meant to be easy, comfortable or a necessarily a majority position. Marion reminds us repeatedly that Christ was certainly in a minority position on the cross (RC, 281; CpV, 52, 112). We should not aim at popularity but at conversion and faithfulness.

In an essay on the resurrection in *Prolegomena to Charity*, Marion returns to this theme. We are to become Christ, Marion insists, imaging and even impersonating Christ as an actor does in a *commedia dell'arte*, a free invention and improvised performance on a known prompt or well-known framework or plot (PC, 144). Yet, here Christ's presence is given as gift in the reality of the church (PC, 130). The disciples receive Christ's blessing, but they also pass it on. Christ disappears in the gesture of blessing (as at Emmaus), precisely so that we might now make the gift visible in us by continuing Christ's blessing. Christ's departure enables the disciples to perform him, to 'become the actors of charity' and to take on the role of Christ (PC, 141). It allows believers to enter into the life of the Trinity: 'If Christ leaves, it is in order to free the trinitarian site for the disciples' (PC, 143). This is accomplished in love: 'The disciples must play the role of Christ by loving each other mutually to the point of making Christ recognizable in them' (PC, 144). Even in their mission the disciples are united as brothers in the trinitarian life opened to them by Christ. Here the Christian believer functions as one of the disciples, as a member of the believing community, as part of the body of Christ. The believers become Christians, become 'Christs', by improvising on the pattern he has established for them – a pattern that culminates in the ultimate kenosis of the cross and is most fully expressed in the sacrament of the Eucharist.

This tension between the essential invisibility and hiddenness of sanctity, on the one hand, and the general call to all baptized believers to become 'Christs', on the other, works out the implications of the saturated phenomenon on a theological level in the lived reality of the believer. The life of faith – that is, the life of discipleship in the community of the church as the body of Christ – is both an encounter with the invisible, excessive, inexpressible holiness of the wholly other and the very mundane, everyday, concrete and fleshly outworking of one's commitment to this community, with all its faults and squabbles. Marion always seeks to hold these two extremes in tension: the utter alterity of the divine who cannot be grasped or expressed in any metaphysical formula, against the concrete manifestation of the divine in Christ's immanence, especially in the suffering on the cross. Similarly the high calling of the Christian life – to participate in the very life of the divine, to become 'gods' – is always held together with the reality of baptism and Eucharist as the bodily participation in an ecclesial community in the daily struggle of living Christ in the world. Although Marion does not use this language here, this surely is also an example of the 'banality' or mundaneness of the saturated phenomenon: the fact that we 'taste and see' and touch mundane things like water and bread and oil, which at the same time come to us as expressions of divine grace and love. They call forth a response to this saturated phenomenon of God's self-giving: an invitation to become entirely devoted to God's gift to us, to become converted into an icon of the divine, to witness to this love to the point of martyrdom. Like the reception of the saturated phenomenon more generally, this is neither purely passive nor entirely active in the usual dichotomy. Rather, as Marion has tried to show for the saturated phenomenon, the initiative lies entirely beyond me and I have no control over it, it comes to me suddenly and surprisingly. In this case the initiative is God's, the call comes from the divine, the event is the gift of grace. Yet, at the same time, the reception of this phenomenon is eminently active and even calls forth great effort: conversion of the self and the world in response to the divine gift. This effort is sustained and finds its height and confirmation in the gift of the sacraments.

4. Eucharist: Sacrament of the gift

The theological topic that has engaged Marion most fully throughout his career is that of the sacraments and especially the Eucharist, to which he has devoted several essays and book chapters. Twice he explicitly engages with the traditional Roman Catholic 'definitions' of sacrament: in an early article included in *God without Being* he defends transubstantiation, and in a later piece he analyses various historical and contemporary interpretations of sacrament, such as its being a visible sign of invisible grace. He takes up the topic again in several other articles, some of which were originally published in *Communio* or presented at conferences and are now collected in *Le croire pour le voir*.

The sacrament on which Marion focuses the most often and which he discusses the most fully is the Eucharist. He returns to this topic again and again. The Eucharist, he suggests, is the very core and centre of theology, because it is the place from which the logos is spoken as given (GWB, 142). The theologian must speak from the point of view of the Eucharist, from the Word that gives itself eucharistically. Marion argues that the Eucharist serves as a hermeneutics for theology; it is the lens through which theology is to be seen and spoken. Within the Eucharist, understanding or even recognition of revelation is given, as in the experience of the disciples in Emmaus when they recognize the risen Christ in the breaking of the bread. In the gesture of breaking and sharing the bread, Christ gives himself to be seen and is manifested. Theologians thus find the appropriate place of interpretation 'only in the Eucharist, where the Word in person, silently, speaks and blesses, speaks to the extent that he blesses' (GWB, 151). In order to hear the text correctly, the ecclesial community must experience conversion by the Word. The bishop therefore functions as the theologian par excellence because he stands in the place of Christ (GWB, 152). The task of the theologian and that of the bishop should not be separated and theology must grow out of the lived experience of the Word by the church. The priest or bishop donates the divine gift of charity to each baptized believer who is in a position of reception vis-à-vis the divine gift communicated in the sacrament. The theologian must 'serve charity' by being 'inscribed in the eucharistic rite opened by the bishop' (GWB, 154). The unfolding of theology occurs along eucharistic lines and in the welcome of the gift of the Word within it. Thus, one can also not really speak of progress in theology, because at stake is always to be converted to the Word via participation in the Eucharist.

While the former essay focuses primarily on the activity of theology, arguing that it should be grounded in the Eucharist, a second essay included in *God without Being* (in the section 'hors-texte'/outside the text) considers what it might mean to explain the Eucharist, to articulate what occurs within the sacrament without betraying the mystery at work in it. The focus of the piece is especially on what constitutes 'presence' within the Eucharist, which Marion identifies, not unsurprisingly, with 'gift'. He considers several terms traditionally used to describe what is present in the Eucharist, such as transubstantiation, transsignification and transfinalization, and argues that, appropriately used, these are not metaphysical terms, because they do not reduce the gift to presence. In fact, in the end it may well make more sense to locate the gift in the species rather than in the community's reception. A merely spiritualized interpretation that locates the sacramentality of the sacrament in the receptive spirit of the community rather than in the elements themselves misses the point. The elements matter and are not mere symbols. Community consciousness can just as much become an idol as the logic of substance and accidents. Marion asserts: 'What the consecrated host imposes, or rather permits, is the irreducible exteriority of the present that Christ makes us of himself in this thing that to him becomes sacramental body. That this exteriority, far from forbidding intimacy, renders it possible in sparing it from foundering in idolatry, can be misunderstood only by those who do not want to open themselves to *distance*' (GWB, 169). And, as in *Idol and Distance*, he continues: 'Only distance, in maintaining a distinct separation of terms (of persons), renders communion possible, and immediately mediates the relation' (GWB, 169). But eucharistic presence must be understood on its own terms rather than be assimilated to a metaphysics of presence. The 'present' in this 'presence' is the gift. This gift exercises its own temporality: it is first memorial and eschatological anticipation, and only then daily viaticum. And past and future are not separated from present in some chronological sequence, but in fact become present within liturgical anamnesis (memory) and eschatological promise. 'The Eucharist anticipates what we will be, will see, will love: *figura nostra*, the figure of what we will be, but above all ourselves, facing the gift that we cannot yet welcome, so, in the strict sense, that we cannot yet figure it' (GWB, 174). In the Eucharist each instant becomes a gift: 'The eucharistic presence comes to us, at each instant, as the gift of that very instant, and, in it, of the body of the Christ in whom one must be incorporated' (GWB, 175). Bread and wine function as the gift of charity in which Christ is given in full abandon. By eating the bread we are assimilated into Christ's body (GWB, 179). The mystical reality of the Eucharist affirms its material and its spiritual dimensions. The 'real' body is Christ's ecclesiastical body, more real even than bread and wine. This requires prayer: eucharistic contemplation means a conversion of the gaze through adoration.

In a later essay, Marion again explicitly takes up traditional eucharistic formulations. Here he wonders about how to define the sacrament more generally, although most examples are drawn from the sacrament of the Eucharist. And he suggests that the sacrament might not only be a concern for theology, as he had insisted in the earlier pieces, but operates its own phenomenality. It is thus possible to examine it phenomenologically and to draw on insight from phenomenology in order to understand it. If the Eucharist concerns visibility and invisibility, then it also concerns phenomenality and manifestation. If the sacrament is defined as a 'visible sign of an invisible grace', then a gap is evident in it between visibility and invisibility. That gap has been articulated in various ways, of which Marion explores three. The first derives from the metaphysics of substance, where the gap between visible and invisible is articulated in terms of substance and accidents. While Marion points to both philosophical and theological problems with this model (such as the transfer of accidents from one substance to another or the question of how Christ's body could be captured in the accidents of a substance), he affirms that the sacrament must give itself visibly as invisible, which means that 'it gives itself without withdrawal to the point of abandon' (CpV, 93). A second model talks about the sacrament as invisible cause of a visible effect. While this model has various problems (the effect also remains invisible), Christ is given visibly in his invisible flesh. Thus, here also it gives itself visibly as invisible and hence 'gives itself without withdrawal to the point of abandon' (CpV, 94). Using the language of semiotics, one can also speak of the sacrament as 'sacred sign'. Yet again, the language of sign is shown to be inadequate but, ultimately, the gap between visible and invisible is crossed as the sacrament 'gives itself without withdrawal to the point of abandon' (CpV, 95). All three, then, ultimately display the same kind of phenomenality.

After briefly summarizing the phenomenology of givenness, Marion suggests that the phenomenality of the sacrament can be defined as a phenomenality of abandon. It gives itself so fully that it is completely abandoned and thus ultimately invisible. The sacrament functions as a manifestation of the Trinity: the Son makes visible the Father in his flesh via the Spirit. This manifestation occurs in the church and through what happens within it: liturgy, prayer, reading of Scripture, sacraments, charisms and so forth. That is to say, God's holiness becomes manifested in our love. In the communion of the faithful, as they are connected to Christ, God is shown. 'The indication and accomplishment of salvation are shown in fact by the universal revelation, therefore by the phenomenalization of all the glory of God' (CpV, 99). In the elements of the Eucharist or other sacramental things, God's grace is manifested and God is shown invisibly. That does not mean that God's glory fully appears but rather that it is fully given and appears to the extent that we can bear it. The excess of the sacrament is phenomenalized in our reception. This reception again is characterized by utter kenosis: 'The phenomenality of what gives itself extends to the givenness of the invisible; in short, it qualifies the sacrament as a phenomenon by full right, although by analogy, because what gives itself gives itself to the point of death and of the death on the Cross, because what gives it gives itself absolutely. Christ gives himself enough so that even the invisible face of the Father can show itself among us' (CpV, 102). The sacrament is hence a genuine phenomenon with full phenomenality.

Indeed, Marion goes even further and argues that the Eucharist is the phenomenon par excellence, the highest and supreme

phenomenon that can serve as a paradigm for all others. It does so
in the mode of the gift. The gift – as we have seen repeatedly and
as he reiterates here – derives from love and puts it to work. The
gift itself is not seen; it requires a 'phenomenology of the invisible'
(CpV, 181). That is to say, it deals with what is unseen and yet
given. Only theology has genuine access to it because it comes
from Revelation and attempts to articulate it. Within theology,
'any gift comes from God and hence the gift of God also gives the
gift in general' (CpV, 182). Marion employs the example of Christ's
conversation with the Samaritan woman at Jacob's well in Sychar
as an illustration of how the gift can be missed (she does not at
first recognize that Christ is offering her the gift of living water,
besides the gift of conversing with her in the first place, which
culturally speaking would have been inappropriate on multiple
levels) and also of how it is accepted as the gift of God's self-
givenness in Christ. To recognize the gift it must be doubled in a
gift of recognition. Christ is the invisible gift of God, which in the
eyes of the world leads to scandal or hatred, but is articulated in the
confession of Christ as the Son of God. The glory of God becomes
visible in the face of Christ, but it does so obscurely – most fully
on the cross. Phenomenality has to be crossed by kenosis (CpV,
188). This kenotic gift culminates in the sacraments, the gifts of
bread and wine, where the gift is perfectly given by being fully
abandoned. It does not remain in presence or subsistence but is
consumed; it remains invisible in its very visibility. The Eucharist
perfectly accomplishes the phenomenon of the gift because it is
entirely emptied of itself and in this self-transparency allows the
giver (Christ and ultimately God) to appear, yet only in kenotic
fashion, thus in perfect givenness. As the eucharistic gift allows us
to see the Father by the Son in the Spirit, so the gift more generally
is recognized when it is possible to envision or aim at the one
who gives it and abandons it fully in 'the essential contingency of
givenness' (CpV, 192). The semi-eucharistic breaking of the bread
in Emmaus similarly identifies the risen Christ to the disciples
(CpV, 202–4). The eucharistic gift in all these cases functions as the
lens for God's self-revelation.

Yet, even more, the eucharistic gift provides the hermeneutic
paradigm for any interpretation of the gift and ultimately for
all givens – from the poor to the saturated. The Eucharist thus
is the phenomenon that supremely challenges the hegemony of

metaphysics and overcomes it definitely. It serves as the paradigmatic case of a saturated phenomenon, is the saturated phenomenon par excellence. And it also shows most profoundly what receiving the saturated phenomenon might mean: it is to receive and accept the abundant gift of love, to become incorporated and transformed within it and, in response, to give oneself as a similar gift of love. Here the phenomenological insights become most fully applied to the theological phenomenon, while this phenomenon also functions as the highest instance or even the paradigm for the more general phenomenological patterns and structures. It is particularly striking that this moment of closest identification of the two registers comes not in a doctrinal statement, but in the description of an experience of worship – that of eucharistic contemplation and participation. If this is 'theology' (rather than, say, philosophy), then it is theology in the mode of liturgical practice and personal experience of adoration. But, in some sense, traditional distinctions between philosophy and theology are erased in this phenomenology of revelation: phenomenology serves as a mode of describing and analysing the experience of faith and worship, while the 'theological' experience serves as a particularly useful example and even model for the phenomenological structures. This identification and mutual implication reaches its height in Marion's 2014 Gifford Lectures on the phenomenon of revelation.

6

Manifesting God

In the preceding chapter, we have already seen Marion engaging religious practices explicitly in a manner that is not solely philosophical, but also already theological. In Marion's earlier work, the philosophical and the theological are at times more explicitly distinguished. While his early contributions to *Communio* could be said to be fairly straightforwardly theological, his work on Descartes is obviously philosophical work in the history of philosophy, although, as we have seen, it already has theological implications and may to some extent even flow from certain theological commitments regarding God's transcendence and incomprehensibility. In his phenomenological work Marion generally claims to be working solely as a philosopher, unfolding the phenomena as they present themselves. And yet his examples are often drawn from Scripture, such as the parable of the last judgement for illustrating the phenomenon of a gift where the recipient is unknown, the parable of the prodigal son to show the undoing of the priority of ontological difference and later the phenomenon of forgiveness, Christ's transfiguration on Mount Tabor as an illustration of the supremely saturated and doubly paradoxical phenomenon of revelation, and so forth. Besides this use of biblical examples, Marion also occasionally comments on the theological implications of aspects of his work, usually pointing out how much further theology would have to go in a discussion of the gift, of revelation, of the phenomenon of the human face or of the incomprehensibility of the human person, but not himself proceeding to such a fuller theological analysis. His 2014 Gifford Lectures are probably

the fullest and most sustained articulation to date of how phenomenology can contribute actively and productively to theology and
what a theological unfolding of this phenomenological contribution might look like. We will therefore examine these lectures in
particular detail in this final chapter, before drawing some general
conclusions about the theological implications of Marion's work.
In this chapter I will roughly follow Marion's own division of the
four lectures, so each section of the chapter corresponds more or
less to one of the lectures (with the exception of summaries of a
previous lecture at the beginning of the next) in the order in which
he delivered them, because they sustain a continuous argument,
although I will occasionally supplement the analysis by connecting
it to other aspects of Marion's work. All four Gifford Lectures focus
on the concept of revelation and the reality of God's self-manifestation. 'Manifesting God' is hence not necessarily something we do,
but something that God does for us. At the same time, however,
it is an analysis of the task of Christian theology today, which is
precisely manifesting God or, maybe more precisely, unfolding how
God becomes manifested. In the first lecture (1), Marion lays out
what he calls the 'aporia' of the concept of revelation, analysing
the origins of the concept and its role in the history of philosophy
and theology. In the second lecture (2), he draws on phenomenological insights in order to develop a more adequate way to speak
of revelation. In the third lecture (3), he focuses on Christ as the
revelation of God and in the final lecture (4), he reflects on the
implications of this way of speaking of revelation for unfolding
how God is revealed as Trinity.

1. Revelation and epistemology

In the first lecture, Marion lays out the history of the concept of
revelation, pointing out that it is a very late term that does not gain
importance in theology until the nineteenth century, although today
it is employed as practically synonymous with theology (GR, 8). In
the early church the term revelation appears only in connection with
eschatology or the apocalypse (as in the Revelation of John). How
did the term gain such importance in theology? Marion begins with
Aquinas, who is one of the first to provide a coherent concept of

revelation, although the way he employs it already points to some of the problems within it. Aquinas distinguishes between reason and revelation, which correspond to two theological approaches. 'Rational' theology, which more or less amounts to philosophy, can investigate God through the use of reason. 'Revealed' theology or 'sacra doctrina', which in some way subsequently becomes theology, receives its insights about God from revelation, especially from the Scriptures. The knowledge about God gained from philosophical or metaphysical theology is an indirect knowledge that relies on what is shown about God from effects, such as the ways in which creation might manifest the creator. It is not knowledge about God as such in the way in which revealed theology provides God's very self-manifestation. Aquinas is fairly clear, in Marion's view, that while metaphysics deals with 'Being as such', it is surpassed by revelation relying on the Scriptures (GR, 11). Yet, this raises the question whether this superior insight is a science, a kind of knowledge. Aquinas wants to say that it is and thus imposes an '*epistemological* interpretation of revelation' (GR, 12). Marion traces this aporia through the subsequent tradition: on the one hand, it is clear that God is the ultimate end of theology and cannot ever be fully known by our finite minds; yet on the other hand, as we can only love what we know, some knowledge of God must be possible. Revelation supplies what is missing in human knowledge. The problem is that this provision of knowledge is read under the parameters of human rationality, which provides the pattern for it. Thus, although revelation is in principle superior to and transcends 'natural' or philosophical knowledge, it becomes subject to it by being thought in the terms and on the conditions of human ways of knowing. Revelation becomes subjugated to epistemology (GR, 14).

Although Marion does not comment on it in this context, we see here clearly a parallel to his censure of the early modern move to subject God to epistemology in the notion of the eternal truths. Already there Marion was anxious to show that knowing God is of a different order of thinking, rather than merely a different mode of philosophical (i.e. metaphysical) knowing. Just as God cannot be subject to human principles of mathematics, geometry and logic, which would ultimately subject the divine to the principle of sufficient reason, so the concept of revelation, if it is to provide genuine access to knowledge of God, cannot be read in terms of standard epistemological parameters. These are simply inadequate for knowing the divine. Revelation must function differently – more like Pascal's third order, which argues for a different way of knowing and the openness to a different kind of evidence altogether.

Marion shows that, for Aquinas, the knowledge of revelation does not rely on philosophy, because it would give philosophers privileged access to the divine, but enters immediately after the 'natural light' of reason (GR, 15). Revealed truths cannot be examined by philosophical reason or natural light, but they help us to know better. Yet that comes back to the same aporia: if revelation is a science similar to philosophical science, then it is subject to the parameters of scientific knowledge and God becomes an object about which this science gives insight. Marion argues that in Aquinas and subsequent thinkers there are actually ultimately three sciences or sources of insight: philosophical theology (i.e. what can be known about God from reason), revelation (i.e. what can be known about God from Scripture and revelation), and the supernatural knowledge achieved from the direct vision of God in the afterlife or possibly by the saints in this life in the highest mystical experience. Yet all three end up functioning on epistemological models. Thus, while their sources might be different, their modes of knowing – that is, their methodology – are ultimately univocal. Furthermore, the knowledge of faith becomes subordinate to the beatific vision. And although revealed theology functions on the model of scientific principles, it actually cannot be fulfilled because it always falls short of knowing God's essence, which remains unknowable. Revelation thus becomes unable to justify itself and is grounded on natural knowledge to the extent that it is knowledge at all. In Marion's view, the entire history of modern theology attempts to validate this further. In Suárez, for example, revealed knowledge becomes even further subjugated to scientific propositions and the relation between theology and philosophy becomes reversed (GR, 21–24). Indeed, Marion attributes 'the decisive moment of the submission of revealed theology to the (onto-theological) constitution of *metaphysica*' to Suárez (GR, 25, note 32). The lack of theology then results from seeing revelation as a science of natural reason.

As we have seen in his work on Descartes, Marion equates this philosophical knowledge, which establishes rigorous parameters of science and the grounding of knowledge, with metaphysics.

Revelation becomes hence grounded on metaphysics. Although it has a special content, its procedures and logic are based on science – that is, on philosophy, which is to say, on metaphysics. Marion suggests, however, that while the Protestant Reformation whole-heartedly embraced this essentially philosophical and metaphysical account of revelation, the Roman Catholic tradition remained more cautious. The Council of Trent does not assimilate revealed knowledge to a science and indeed hardly uses the term at all. In the first Vatican Council, the authority for knowledge of revealed things comes not from human reason but from God's authority. Suárez's conclusions are thus indirectly rejected. Even in the Second Vatican Council, which speaks far more explicitly of revelation, it is not seen as an extension of science, but rather as God's self-manifestation. It is hence not read in epistemological terms. 'Natural' knowledge is included in supernatural knowledge or revelation, appealing to Romans 1.19–20, which speaks of anyone having knowledge of God from creation. Marion claims that this verse means not that there is an independent natural knowledge of God that somehow precedes revelation, but rather that it is already part of revelation and hence comprised within it (GR, 28–29). God is manifested and revealed even to the 'natural' light. Revelation thus *itself* produces and unfolds knowledge; it need not and should not be submitted to epistemological parameters imported from a different discipline and a foreign realm of science. God is known via the divine self-revelation in love. We have returned to the order of charity, but in considerably more elaborated fashion than in Pascal or even in Marion's own earlier work.

Marion reiterates this argument at the start of the second lecture. The separation between reason and faith in modern theology creates a curious paradox that allows theology both to posit itself as a rational, scientific enterprise, but at the same time to claim superiority over the other sciences as their 'queen'. Yet, this claimed scientificity is imprecise and invalidated by the inaccessibility of the beatific vision. Thus revelation ultimately becomes submitted to scientific categories. Marion cites several examples here: Hume, Locke, Rousseau, Kant, Fichte and others all make theology subject to metaphysics. Reason becomes 'natural revelation' that must be submitted to critique (Kant) or contained in a 'concept' (Hegel). The limits of reason end up showing that Scripture is irrational (Spinoza, Hume) or must be reformulated in rational terms (Kant).

Thus, we see the logical outcome of making revelation subject to epistemological parameters: because this kind of rationality can only know objects and the infinite cannot be comprehended within the limits of the finite, it becomes ultimately excluded from reason altogether. Religion either is confined 'within the limits of reason alone' or simply dismissed as fideism and superstition.

A development can be perceived in this progress of subjecting revelation to the parameters of rational, philosophical knowing, just as Marion had earlier traced a history of successive idolatrous concepts for the divine. At first it becomes pushed from the realm of science (e.g. the rejection of miracles) or ontology (e.g. the refutation of proofs for God's existence), but survives in the realm of morality. Revelation becomes interpreted in purely ethical terms: God can be known as the moral legislator of the universe. Hegel tries to inscribe the absolute in the field of knowing in a different way by advancing an alternate concept of the infinite. He distinguishes between 'revealed' (*geoffenbarte*) and 'revealing' (*offenbare*) knowledge and reminds of the original relationship between revelation and eschatology (GR, 33). Although this is a step in the right direction, in Hegel it remains inscribed in the activity of reason and absolute spirit as the arbiter of truth. The real character of revelation is always masked when it is understood as a truth based on evidence. Although Marion does not here speak of this in terms of idolatry or the 'death of God', he is clearly reiterating his claims about a continuous history of inadequate concepts for the divine, which are metaphysical in character precisely because they make God subject to human concepts. Revelation must instead be unfolded from itself and analysed in the way in which it actually manifests itself.

2. Revelation and phenomenology

Marion argues that we must free revelation from its epistemological constrictions, imposed on it by modernity, and instead think of it in different terms. Reason and revelation do not pursue the same operations. Instead revelation must be explicated and unfolded from itself and according to its own inherent logic (GR, 34). Marion here appeals to Heidegger, who reconnects – even more fully than Hegel – truth (*aletheia*) to apocalypse. Truth is not about 'clear and distinct' evidence as Descartes and most of modernity claimed, but instead about the unfolding of what has been covered over (*lethe* means to cover up or hide, hence *a-letheia*, truth, etymologically speaking can be interpreted as an uncovering or a kind of revealing). Instead of subjecting it to the principle of contradiction and the principle of sufficient reason, truth must be based on conditions of possibility (GR, 35). Marion suggests that we go back to the original definition of revelation in terms of 'apocalypse' and explore the implications of this more fully as a possibility of freeing it from the metaphysical constrictions modernity imposed on it.

Marion draws on Pascal again here by arguing that charity plays the role of a condition of knowledge for what is inaccessible and impossible by suggesting that the will might have its own kind of evidence that 'commands' the understanding. Here, however, the will is explicitly connected to the work of the Spirit: the Holy Spirit must teach us in our hearts, according to the order of charity, the knowledge of the heart. This is an alternative kind of reason that operates via 'attraction' of the will. The desire for God then leads to experience of the divine and knowledge of God. Marion claims that this is supported by the psalms, in which desire for God or pleasure in God is portrayed as fulfilled in a kind of knowledge of God. He suggests that this 'attraction' of desire is precisely the logic of love. A theological understanding of revelation then has two characteristics. On the one hand, it relies on the attraction or love between Father and Son. We can only will if we love what we desire and this desire and will is ultimately received from God. The will then decides reason to see; we believe *in order to* see, but the desire itself comes from elsewhere and is ultimately a gift of God. On the other hand, this understanding of revelation allows us to see Jesus as the Christ, as the visibility of the invisible (GR, 41). As in Marion's earlier work, this is not an insight of science but an insight of the will: I must want to interpret Jesus as the Christ. It hence requires a hermeneutic decision. Again, one must believe in order to see.

As in the fourth chapter of his book on Augustine's *Confessions*, Marion thus establishes the following relation, which he also sees in some other medieval thinkers (he cites St Thierry as an example): the desire to believe leads to love, which provides a kind of knowledge, but all three – desire, love, knowledge – are gifts of God. When the will is oriented toward Christ, it gains in understanding. One understands more as one loves Christ more. We can see what is unfolded or uncovered in revelation only if we love (GR, 43). Knowing, then, amounts to loving, and faith is this knowledge of love. Love only knows, however, if it can govern its own conditions. It begins in God. Revelation is thus self-revelation of God. It is revelation in the sense of apocalypse. To work this out, Marion appeals again, as he has before, to the difference between two kinds of reason, two kinds of logos, two kinds of wisdom, as Paul contrasts them in his letters: the wisdom of the world and the wisdom of God. While the wisdom of God appears as folly to the world, it is not simply illogical, but a *different* kind of logic (GR, 46). Our standard conception of logic, Marion claims, does not rule over every kind of logos, but can be transformed 'by the logic of *the* Logos' (GR, 47), Christ. We must therefore pay attention to how this logos is manifested. Because it is a matter of manifestation, we can take recourse to phenomenology to analyse its mode of manifestation. That does not mean that we are imposing foreign philosophical parameters upon it – as Marion had contended modern theology does by adopting metaphysical paradigms – but revelation appears as manifestation and hence is already inherently phenomenological. To unfold how it manifests itself is to depict it as it gives itself instead of constituting it in a priori fashion.

The logos is then not phenomenalized on the basis of the gaze, as in Husserlian phenomenology. It is not subject to a priori concepts or the synthesis of a transcendental subject. Rather, it gives itself and hence must be allowed to appear on its own terms. We do not owe its appearing to the Kantian conditions of possibility of phenomena for a transcendental ego, but instead must pay attention to how it appears on its own terms. The phenomenon of revelation gives itself and must be received as such. It comes from itself as an event, as a saturated phenomenon. That means, however, that it does enter phenomenology, that it can be phenomenalized, and hence that an account can be given of it, as long as it is allowed to unfold from itself and on its own terms. Christ gives himself in a full phenomenon: he comes among us but from himself, on his own initiative. The phenomenalization goes even beyond death, because Christ gives and takes up his life again (GR, 49). This phenomenon is recognized most clearly in the biblical texts. How does the resurrected Christ appear as a phenomenon? Marion suggests that three characteristics can be ascertained from its self-revelation.

First, such a phenomenon displays an *excess of intuition* over the concept or over signification. It gives too much and hence cannot be constituted starting from the intentionality of a transcendental subject. Marion points to the other categories of saturated phenomena he has explored (event, idol, flesh, icon) to stress that they are imposed without comprehension or signification being imposed on them. They designate the reality of the impossible to come from itself. There are no words or concepts for these phenomena, we are blinded and left without voice. The saturated phenomenon is so intense that it overwhelms our normal parameters of rationality and cannot be explained by or within them. Instead Christ must provide his own meaning and signification as he does, for example, for the disciples on the road to Emmaus or at the Sea of Tiberias, instances where, Marion insists repeatedly, the signification and unveiling always comes '*from elsewhere*' (GR, 52). They do not recognize him and have no concepts for what has happened. The meaning of the event, its signification, must come to them from elsewhere. Similarly, Mary Magdalene does not recognize the risen Christ by his voice, thinking him to be the gardener. Only when he speaks her name, gives her a name instead of receiving one from her, does she realize it is Christ speaking to her.

Second, then, the one who encounters Christ is no longer a constituting transcendental subject but becomes a *witness* (GR, 52). The recipient of the phenomenon can no longer anticipate it via intentionality. There are no concepts that would apply to the phenomenon in advance as is true for objects where the aim of the subject makes them visible and determines their knowledge. In the case of objects, intentionality is superior to intuition because the subject imposes concepts on the object and understands it within predetermined parameters. The saturated phenomenon makes this impossible. No concepts are adequate; no synthesis is possible. The witness *knows* but does not *comprehend* – what is given cannot be unified in a concept or identified in a signification. For example, the blind man Christ heals at the pool of Siloam acknowledges the fact of healing but never pretends to comprehend it. This stature of the witness then becomes the normal and inevitable posture of anyone who encounters phenomena of revelation. The true signification comes not from the witness, but only the event itself spurs belief (GR, 55).

Third, the phenomenon of revelation is shown to function as a *paradox* and to be experienced in terms of *counter-experience*. Marion insists that this is not a matter of a logical contradiction or an empirical impossibility or a mere obscurity that could be clarified with further research, but something that comes to us or occurs precisely by undoing the conditions of experience. By undoing the finite conditions of experience, it becomes a logical category for saturated phenomena and a way of allowing the things themselves to appear from themselves. This paradox extends and enlarges experience. God's self-manifestation is radically imposed. God irrupts within the finite, which cannot contain or see the infinite, but this very rupture leaves marks (GR, 57). The apocalypse begins in Christ and comes without conditions. It is ultimately a manifestation of such radical holiness that it can only be received by dying, which becomes the condition of reception itself. The point is not whether this phenomenon contradicts the normal conditions of knowing, but *how* it does so. It is still a case of phenomenality, but this radical phenomenality must be described on its own terms as the 'counter-experience of Revelation' or as the 'paradigmatic saturated phenomenon' (GR, 59). Consequently, because we cannot endure the excess of evidence given to us and must nevertheless bear witness to it, we require the Spirit to open the path and the method of interpretation for us. Furthermore, this phenomenality and its interpretation are always expressed in charity. Marion appeals to Ephesians 3.17-19, which speaks of the immensity of God's charity, to argue that 'the phenomenon of Revelation is both saturated and saturating: *charity*' (GR, 60). This, he concludes, frees the concept of revelation anew for theology.

Marion is hence here clearly employing his phenomenological parameters of a phenomenology of givenness and the saturated phenomenon for explicating biblical revelation, implicitly arguing that phenomenology is a more adequate tool for theology than metaphysics or the philosophy of modernity. He explicitly says that it does greater justice to the biblical texts and the ways in which they portray the experience of revelation. The characteristics he outlines here – the excess of intuition over the concept or over signification, the 'I' being turned into the witness of the phenomenon that comes in surprising and unpredictable fashion, the notion of counter-experience or paradox – are all central aspects of his general phenomenology of givenness. That is how all saturated phenomena give themselves. The phenomenon of revelation then emerges as a more intense and excessive version of other sorts of manifestation. Phenomenology allows us access to God's self-revelation in Christ because it allows the phenomenon to unfold itself freely rather than imposing epistemological parameters upon it. Marion argues throughout that phenomenological parameters do not inflict the same constrictions or subversion on revelation precisely because they are not prefabricated, but seek to be completely attentive to how the phenomenon is actually given and experienced.

3. Revelation and Christ

In this context, however, Marion goes further. He argues not only for the greater adequacy of phenomenology for giving a philosophical account of revelation, but proceeds to draw out explicitly theological implications. These are in line with what he has said in more theologically oriented articles, yet his treatment here is far more fully connected to the phenomenological insights. In the third lecture he justifies this in terms of several biblical passages that speak of the mysteries of the kingdom. Although God uncovers the mystery to anyone who wishes to see it and hence the phenomenon of revelation is freely given to all, not all are ready to receive it. Only those who are willing to hear or understand are given to see and receive. The mystery of revelation comes to us (at least in the synoptic gospels) as an event of the kingdom. It is an unforeseeable, unrepeatable, unpredictable, impossible phenomenon. The kingdom is happening as an incomprehensible and obscure glory, as a 'doxa' that turns the standard opinions upside down, hence as a 'para-dox' (doxa in Greek can designate both 'glory' and 'opinion'). The mystery of revelation hence always requires proclamation and reception. In this proclamation the order of manifestation is inverted: it is recognition that provokes knowledge, believing that allows for seeing and understanding.

Truth is un-covered or dis-covered. What does the mystery give in this phenomenalization? How does this un-covering or dis-covery work? And what is it that is un-covered or dis-covered? These are the three questions Marion tries to answer in the third lecture.

He draws on Paul again in order to examine the question of what is phenomenalized in the mystery of God. Paul speaks of it: (a) as a 'secret wisdom'; (b) as not only wisdom but also charity; and (c) as charity revealed in the gaze of Christ. It is a secret wisdom because it is not a worldly wisdom but instead a mystery that lies within the depths of God. It must be revealed to us by the Spirit of God. We must receive it in our hearts by learning to see as God sees. This requires a shift of the point of view; it overturns intentionality and tries to see from God's gaze, from God's point of view. Marion draws on the figure of anamorphosis to depict this conversion of the gaze where I learn to have the mind of Christ, the mind of the Spirit. 'God's intentionality, God's interpretation, God's constitution of his own phenomenon' becomes determinate (GR, 65), as in the eucharistic hermeneutic outlined in *God without Being*. This divine 'interpretation' is learned through the conversion of the gaze in the counter-experience. But this inter-pretation can be received only as it is given by the Spirit. In Paul's letters, this creates a 'conflict of interpretations' between the secret wisdom of God and Greek wisdom, which Marion interprets in terms of the philosophy of being, hence metaphysics. Metaphysical 'wisdom' either seeks God negatively as 'being' or as 'dead' or it relies on signs, but even these signs are always subject to our power. This constitutes a refusal of conversion. Conversion instead means a radical turning, a rupture in rationality itself. The logos of the world becomes replaced by the logos of the cross. The power of the gospel is that we see the mystery uncovered in the gaze of the logos. It seems like folly or stupidity to those who do not want to see it, but in reality this judgement comes from the refusal to change the point of view and is a self-deception and a denial of the evidence. Marion already said to Jocelyn Benoist, who had argued that where Marion sees God most people see nothing, that this is not because there is nothing there to be seen, but because the observer is blind and denies the evidence of God's self-revelation (VR, 124). One must learn to see otherwise via a conversion of the gaze.

The divide between a phenomenology of intentionality and a phenomenology of givenness, then, turns on the anamorphosis, the point of view. The standpoint for the anamorphosis that enables seeing the phenomenon of revelation as it gives itself is learnt from the teaching of the Spirit. For Greek philosophy, or for any metaphysical philosophy, God should unfold in the realm of being and uphold the distinction between being and non-being. But, according to Paul, passages Marion had already cited to a similar effect in *God without Being*, the distinction between being and non-being is erased and overturned by God who hence undoes ontological distinctions. God's point of view turns everything upside down (GR, 69). The difference between ontic and ontological is set aside. God overturns death with life via resurrection and creation, in which ontological difference is cancelled. The being of things depends on God's power: nothing is anything by itself but only because God grants it the gift of life.

This is not only a secret wisdom, but it is the wisdom of charity. Marion here carries further his interpretation of the passage from Ephesians that speaks of the manifestation to the saints of God's riches in terms of charity. The horizon of being is displaced by the horizon of charity. Only charity is truly hyperbolic, unconditioned and indescribable. The gaze of charity does not identify, constitute or define, but instead recognizes or acknowledges the excess of charity that saturates the gaze. This charity transcends the world, which Marion sees illustrated by the fact that it features four dimensions instead of the usual three: Paul speaks of the breadth and length and height and depth of God's mystery in the love of Christ (Eph. 3.18-19). The immensity of this love transcends the world and enters into a 'divine milieu' (GR, 71). It is not a space before me, but a space in which I find myself: I experience saturation as it encompasses me in a way that is irreducible to other phenomena because infinitely multiplied.

How, then, is this mystery of revelation phenomenalized? Most fundamentally, it comes from the gaze of Christ, whose gaze is the only one that is not finite. As Paul points out, all is recapitulated in Christ. Christ is able to see with an infinite gaze, but he does so from within our flesh. The mystery of charity operates in the gaze of Christ. The mystery of Christ is the mystery of God. Via charity we have access to God in Christ. He fulfils the law in his flesh. God reconciles us in Christ as Christ recapitulates all in himself. In Christ the mystery of peace appears once and for all 'as the unique phenomenalization of the Father'; Christ functions as the 'phenomenal center of the glory of all things' (GR, 74). All givenness comes from Christ, all visibility returns to him, because he is the icon of the invisible God, the visible image of God's invisible splendour and glory.

This leads Marion to the second question: How does this un-covering give itself? What is the *operation* of the apocalypse? The mystery is hidden and hence must be manifested as the reverse of the unseen. It is ground for apocalypse or revelation (GR, 75). Marion formulates the principle that he thinks governs the phenomenality of revelation as examined so far, namely a proportional relationship between mystery and apocalypse: as there is more mystery, there is correspondingly more revelation. For God, the hidden becomes manifest in the advent of Christ. He is the fund or ground of the unseen and becomes the possibility for manifestation. Christ manages to render the mystery phenom-enalized as such, to manifest it concretely without doubling it. The phenomenon shows itself from itself as it gives itself. Only in Christ is this fully accomplished, because Christ is both the phenomenon and its mode of manifestation. Christ gives himself entirely, loves to the very end, to the 'it is finished' on the cross. He manifests the phenomenon entirely from itself. Christ is hence the supreme manifestation, the 'phenomenon of all phenomena'; he is 'the total and saturating agent of the putting into evidence of the absolute unseen' (GR, 77). He makes manifest everything else. Yet, it depends on us whether Christ's manifestation will become manifest in Christ's presence. Our decision matters for revelation to become manifested fully.

Marion stresses that without Christ we cannot understand, but that we must respond to his call. He points to passages in all three synoptic gospels that speak of what is hidden becoming manifest. In Mark 4.22 the mystery of the kingdom comes to those who have listened to the call and who have become Christ's disciples. They must take on Christ's point of view. In Luke 8.17, the lamp that shows everything designates the hermeneutic figure of the witness, which requires a radical listening even if one does not fully under-stand. Hearing and doing the logos go together: how one hears determines how one welcomes and proclaims. The hearer must become witness and proclaim the gospel. To understand Christ is to enter into the mystery. Christ then becomes less comprehensible to those who do not want to understand. For example, in the

Scriptures the Pharisees and Herod refuse to change interpretations and to pass over to the mystery's point of view and hence do
not see or understand Christ. In Matthew 10.26 the manifestation
concerns the link between refusing the kingdom and the ensuing
incomprehensibility. The unintelligibility of the parables results
precisely from the decision to reject Christ and refuse the coming
of the kingdom. The shift to a different point of view is accomplished through the grace of God. The un-covering happens from
the Father in Christ via the activity of the Spirit. We must accept
this gift of the Father. When he acknowledges Jesus as the Messiah,
Peter 'allows himself to be placed in the very place of its phenomenalization, the trinitarian site opened by the Spirit between the
Father and the Son' (GR, 82). The second question regarding the
'how' of phenomenalization is hence answered via anamorphosis:
we must shift to the viewpoint of the witness and with the aid of
the Spirit see Christ from the Father's stance.

The third question Marion addresses in this lecture concerns
what is un-covered and *who* is shown in the truth of revelation. He
focuses this in terms of the question of hermeneutics. The divide
between flesh and Spirit has to be crossed hermeneutically and this
is granted by God. We must enter into this particular hermeneutic
circle, where God offers both the phenomenon and the conditions for seeing it. Christ is seen if access to the phenomenon of
revelation is granted by the Father. To see Jesus as the Christ refers
to the Father in a doubled fashion: on the one hand, the Father
establishes Christ's condition and we must see him from his point
of view; on the other hand, the Father is the very 'ground of the
unseen' (GR, 84). The Father is seen in the Son, but the Son is given
by the Father. Christ is seen as Son correspondingly more fully
as he is referred to the Father who gives him. Christ acts not for
and out of himself but actually 'inauthentically', like the saturated
phenomenon. Christ acts from anamorphosis: he completely takes
God's point of view. (Marion points out that only Satan speaks
from his own point of view.) Christ's absolute self-referral without
remainder to the Father shows the trinitarian place and centre of
revelation. Christ is the icon of the invisible God. To see Christ is
to see the Father (GR, 85).

This is hence also a phenomenality of the gift: Christ is shown
forth as gift, as Son. Doing the will of the Father is taking his
point of view. Believing becomes seeing. The anamorphosis of

faith repeats the trinitarian anamorphosis. Only in this way can
we interpret the Father's voice that manifests the Son, for example
at Christ's baptism and transfiguration. Christ makes manifest the
Father and confirms his glory. This glory is shown via a manifestation of the Trinity and helps us enter into the Trinity. This is
encapsulated in love: the Father loves and whoever loves Christ is
loved by the Father and included in the trinitarian game of love.
The Trinity, as Marion explores more fully in the final lecture, is
the place of un-covering, of revelation. In the Trinity we see what
shows itself by receiving what gives itself from itself, namely by
receiving ourselves from God who also gives us the condition for
seeing and reception (GR, 88).

In this third lecture Marion hence goes much further than he
does in his previous work. Although he had obviously already
frequently spoken of Christ as the icon of the Father, interpreting
this to mean that he is the visible image of the invisible God, he
explicates this much more fully here and relies much more heavily
on biblical texts for unfolding the meaning of this revelation of
God by Christ in the Spirit. The revelation of God in Christ occurs
through the mystery of the kingdom, made present among us in
Christ's ministry but accepted as such only by those willing to
acknowledge him as the face of the invisible God, as the Messiah/
Christ. Marion had already in God without Being argued that the
theologian must pass over to God's point of view, that theo-logy
means to speak from the theos. He also had explicated this in
hermeneutic terms: Christ provides the right interpretation of the
mystery of God in the gift of love of the Eucharist. Hermeneutics
proceeds from the point of view of the Word. Instead of designating
what we arbitrarily impose on the phenomenon, hermeneutics is
what is given to us as gift. Yet, here this hermeneutics is qualified
much more fully. Speaking from God's point of view does not
constitute some sort of privileged standpoint, which we can assume
through an act of will or which might happen automatically in the
Eucharist. Rather, explicating this 'point of view' via anamorphosis
means that it is an attitude of reception that puts itself in the place
assigned to it through conversion. To speak from Christ's point of
view means precisely to become completely devoted to the gift as it
is given and to recognize even the capacity to receive it as a gift.

Yet, what is maybe most novel about Marion's explorations
of these themes in the Gifford Lectures is the heavily trinitarian

language. Although he has obviously mentioned the Trinity in other places and certainly does not ignore it when speaking of Christ, the unfolding of revelation as most essentially trinitarian is a much more explicitly theological development of his previous work. These trinitarian dimensions are worked out most fully in the fourth and final lecture.

4. Revelation and the Trinity

In the final lecture, Marion discusses the logic of God's manifestation as it is revealed in the reality of the Trinity. He argues that a phenomenological approach to the 'good news' is able to unfold its moments of uncovering that are previously covered over. Via the saturated phenomenon and the hyperbole of charity as it is evidenced in Christ, we can be led to a recognition of the Father who makes us a witness of Christ in Jesus. Thus we see the invisible Father in the visible Son. Christ himself is the paradox of Revelation and hence the Trinity is phenomenologically accessible. It is not an obscure theological doctrine, but the essential 'place encompassing the phenomenological dimensions of the uncovering... of the visible icon of the invisible God' (GR, 90). Marion warns that there are various dangers here, well known from the history of theology: a politicizing of the Trinity, the fall into tritheism, and so forth. Christianity, Marion suggests, brings together the unicity and the unity of God in a particular way. While Judaism and Islam think unicity on the basis of unity, Christianity thinks unity on the basis of unicity (GR, 91). Marion claims that it must do so, because in Christianity God's identity is most supremely articulated in terms of love and hence must operate in the form of communion: God's identity is a unity of love. The unity of communion in God is thus not a mathematical unicity; the Trinity is not about counting from one to three. Marion suggests that the phenomenality of un-covering that he has laid out in the previous lecture should be able to corroborate the unity of God and make it manifest as Triune. The 'unity of the communion of the trinitarian terms' must be able to 'appear as a phenomenon' (GR, 91). The Trinity is hence not about some abstract transcendence of God, but about God's very immanence, about the Father's self-revelation in the Son through the Spirit.

Marion returns to the distinction between natural and super-natural knowledge he had explored in the initial lecture and claims that this distinction became superimposed (at least in Western theology) on the distinction between the one God, who can be known via natural knowledge or philosophy, and the Trinity, to which one has access only via revelation. Thus how God is known becomes divided into two modes of knowledge or two sciences, which correspond to God's unity and God's Trinity respectively and amount to a distinction between God's essence and God's existence. This is, as Marion had stressed in the first lecture, an epistemological distinction. Natural reason knows the unity of essence, but has no access to the Trinity of persons, which is known only via revelation. This division of the divine substance into two parts means that the Trinity no longer has anything to do with the essence of God, which can be known philosophically, although the terminology of substance was not always fully embraced. The relation between the divine unity and the persons of the Trinity is often unclear in the tradition. Kant, for example, ultimately judges the doctrine of the Trinity as completely irrelevant and in that respect becomes determinative for many others: the plurality of God is useless for reason, and strict monotheism requires setting aside the doctrine of the Trinity. Marion thinks that Hegel, Nietzsche and Heidegger all remain within this philosophical horizon, in which God becomes thinkable without trinitarian communion. Although twentieth-century theology sought to overcome this (somewhat differently in Rahner and Barth), Marion judges the distinction between the 'economic' and the 'immanent' Trinity not particularly successful.

Instead, he suggests, we must think revelation on the basis of the Trinity. The mode of God's self-manifestation or un-covering is trinitarian. Only the Trinity can reveal the Trinity (GR, 99). The Trinity designates precisely God's self-revelation of both content and mode. The *mode* of manifestation is equivalent to the *what* of manifesting. The economy of God's self-revelation is not a linear history. Rather, it comes as a saturated phenomenon of the event. There are no concepts that could grasp it, but it arrives as a surprise and imposes an infinite hermeneutics. These are not successive historical revelations in some chronological fashion. Rather, they function on the model of the phenomenality of the Trinity: unicity is thought in terms of unity and unity means union through communion, not through mathematical addition (GR, 101). Love is here determinative: the plurality is the very condition of the unity. Marion claims that the more relation there is, the more love enables a unity in the communion. We thus should not start from the immanent Trinity (Rahner) or the monarchy of the Father, but must describe *our* access to the un-covering of what remains essentially inaccessible.

The Trinity, Marion contends, manifests itself according to the logic of the icon. He refers to passages in Basil, Gregory Nazianzen and Augustine to support this. The icon is essential in all of them. Basil argues in a striking passage that a king and his icon are both the same and different. The icon makes the invisible king visibly present – but it is not the icon that is primary, rather the visibility of the icon bears on another and passes to another. It is a 'visible with a double effect' by referring to another who would otherwise remain invisible (GR, 103). The same logic works for the trinitarian model. Christ is the icon of the invisible God. Whoever sees Christ sees not just the visible Jesus, but the invisible God. The identity of persons is uncovered in the process of manifestations as shared. The revelation of the Trinity is thus unfolded in an iconic manner. By being put into an icon, the face of the Son has to be seen in a particular way in order to see in it the face of God. It is a 'visibility with a double entry' (GR, 104). Yet, how can this iconic visibility be accomplished? It requires the work of the Spirit. The grace, gift, art and manner of seeing are given by the Spirit. The Holy Spirit shows the icon and therefore remains invisible. (Marion cites several biblical and patristic passages to support this.) The Holy Spirit, then, has the 'invisible and indispensable function' of working the 'phenomenal (iconic) model of the Trinity'.

But this is a phenomenological model that must be received and phenomenalized, which is our task. The Spirit deifies us through the Son's incarnation. The Spirit has a doubled phenomenological function. On the one hand, Jesus is the revelatory instance of the Father only by and through the work of the Spirit. The Spirit functions as the revealing or developing agent who makes Christ's face visible as the face of God. On the other hand, the Spirit works on us to enable us to see this phenomenological mode. The Spirit gives the power to see the truth, gives the full knowledge of it and shows the glory of God. The Spirit helps us see the face of Christ and to discern there the invisible gaze of the Father. Marion calls

this 'the trinitarian method of "putting into an icon"' (GR, 108).
Thus, the Spirit works the anamorphosis by positioning our gaze
and putting us in the right place for seeing. The Spirit functions
as the 'axis' (GR, 108) of the meeting of gazes of Christ and
the Father, but also of the human and the divine. While we are
usually focused on a spectacle, the Spirit overturns our normal
'phenomenal arrangement' and helps us move to anamorphosis,
places us at the site necessary for recognition. The Spirit stages the
glory of the Father and reveals the depths of God. The Spirit is not
a 'third spectacle' or a second incarnation, but rather operates the
one visible (GR, 109). The Spirit bears the stamp of the Father in
the Son and seals us with it in baptism. The Spirit, then, provides
the condition of seeing the one visibility.

The Spirit is also the operator of holiness and sanctification. This
is not an ontic but a 'phenomenal model of the Trinity' (GR, 110),
which Marion claims is confirmed by Augustine. Christ shows the
Father. In Augustine, the invisible Father and the invisible Spirit
become visible in the Son. The invisible communion is manifested
in the Son. The gap between the visible and the invisible is thus
within the Trinity; it does not have to be externalized to become
a phenomenon. The Spirit remains invisible and does not appear
except as the gift of love within God, the gift of Son and Father
together. The Spirit is the complete phenomenalization of the gift
and of giving. The Spirit is the complete phenomenon of the gift,
because the Spirit 'gives giving, giving in itself' (GR, 113). The
Spirit eternally proceeds as gift and is always giving, even before
becoming gift. The Spirit is hence essentially giveable, *what* the
Spirit gives coincides with the process of giving. In this self-giving,
the Spirit gives God. Marion claims that the Spirit does not appear
because the very phenomenality of the gift as perfect abandonment
without return forbids it. The gift is fully received and hence giver
and gift disappear. The Spirit gives to see but is not seen. Even in
teaching us to pray, the Spirit is heard but not seen. There are thus,
Marion says, 'three operators of its manifestation, three works of
its revelation' (GR, 115): the invisible Father in the visible face of
the Son via the anamorphosis worked by the Spirit. Revelation
occurs '*from* the Spirit *through* the Son *to* the Father' (GR, 114).
In this way God's self-revelation is seen from the viewpoint of
manifestation, ultimately from our viewpoint. This is the viewpoint
of confession, not of theological formula.

Thus, if theology were to take phenomenology seriously, it might discover a way of unfolding the mystery of God from the ways in which it is actually experienced, as documented in the Scriptures, the tradition, the lives of the saints, in our own encounter with the risen Word in the sacraments, without taking recourse to an abstract philosophical system that would impose a foreign logic on revelation. Marion contends that revelation is best understood from within itself, on its own terms and according to its own logic, which does not require the rationality of the sciences and of technology. This does not render it irrational or incomprehensible, but instead understands it within the logic of love, which is a logic of manifestation, rather than in a logic of economy or reproduction. Theology certainly must think through the gift of God, but it need not thereby think it mathematically or geometrically or scientifically. Rather, it must give as rigorously as possible an account of the ways in which God is manifested and revealed. God's own manifestation, then, governs theology, our manifesting of the divine manifestation.

Phenomenology, then, enables the articulation of the phenomenon of revelation in a way that is much more compelling than past distinctions between natural and supernatural knowledge about God or other such metaphysical analyses. It also shows itself as a particularly appropriate and useful language for unfolding the given of revelation in the Scriptures and the lived tradition. At the same time, revelation emerges as the givenness par excellence, and thus as able to accomplish the very essence of phenomenality, as Marion claims in the introduction to the printed version of the Gifford Lectures (GR, 7). The 'examples' of theology can therefore contribute to the phenomenological exploration by showing ways in which givenness is especially successfully manifested in particular experiences.

At the same time, Marion's analysis of revelation in the Gifford Lectures is considerably more 'abstract' and 'technical' than his more confessional writings for *Communio* (which are obviously addressed to a different audience). His exposition of the history of the concept of revelation and his application of phenomenological categories to a more 'apocalyptic' notion of revelation is articulated almost entirely in a systematic register, showing their alternative rationality and internal logic, and does not address the life of faith or the sacraments head-on, as we saw him do in the texts discussed in the previous chapter. Yet, these two treatments are certainly not incompatible or contradictory to each other. Revelation is most fully manifested and completely given in the texts that witness to God's mystery and in the gift of the Spirit's teaching. Using the phenomenological categories of the saturated phenomenon and the phenomenology of givenness more generally enables us not only to articulate and unfold this theologically, but also to experience it and thus to become a devoted witness to the divine revelation. It helps us to guard against attempting to constitute the divine manifestation, to govern over it as a subject or to predict and limit it. Instead it teaches us a more appropriate response: to witness to the invisible unseen and to devote ourselves to it in love, unfolding its revelation not only as it comes to us but also as it is increasingly manifested in the witness of our lives, if we are willing to receive it and allow the Spirit to guide us.

Conclusion

What are the implications of Marion's philosophy for theology?
His work obviously can be made to answer systematic questions
or be analysed in systematic terms. One might say that his 'christ-
ology' is deeply marked by kenosis, by Christ's utter self-givenness
in love. Christ, for Marion, is the visible face of the invisible
Father who reveals God to us through his death on the cross.
God becomes visible as pure gift of love in Christ, especially in
Christ's willingness to absorb evil instead of passing it on. Marion's
'soteriology' is characterized by this kenotic self-abandon in love
for the sinner who does not deserve it. Yet, it effects deification:
its utter abnegation is combined with a confident belief that we
may become gods and participate in the divine if we take on the
face of Christ and continue his mission of making God present in
and through the gift of love. This soteriology has profound implications also for 'anthropology': the human, to some extent like
the divine, is essentially incomprehensible. The imago dei, interpreted in terms of God's incomprehensibility, forbids any reductive
definition or use of the human. As Christ functions as icon of the
invisible God, so the human can and should function as icon of
Christ. To be genuinely human is to be a god. But to be God is
to die – in the complete self-emptying on the cross. This is linked
to what one might call Marion's 'hamartiology'; he speaks of the
continual passing on of pain, hurt and evil, which is only stopped
in Christ's willingness to endure and absorb pain and evil and
thereby allow the cycle of violence and revenge to end in him. Sin
consists in not recognizing the divine gifts but spurning them and

appropriating them as possession (NC, 41). Conversion means not only to recognize and receive the gift of God but to love in the same kenotic fashion that refuses to pass on evil and instead is willing to absorb it by love. Just as God is most fundamentally defined by infinite, boundless, overwhelming and, above all, unconditioned love, so such love calls forth a response in us. Receiving God's love means to live like Christ, to make him present, by being continually converted to him in love and by giving oneself as gift, just as he gave himself. This constitutes at the same time what might be read as Marion's 'ecclesiology': deeply marked by the Eucharist, the church is called to be continually converted into the body of Christ through the work of the Spirit and to convert the world. This is what can be said about 'pneumatology': it is the Spirit who makes us into an image of Christ, who allows us a glimpse of the invisible, who serves as the breath of the call from the divine. And one may even point to eschatological implications: we must speak of eternity and even resurrection of the body, because faithfulness to the unfathomlessness of the other allows for no less.

We *can* make Marion speak on all these systematic topics or even attempt to shape these implications into some sort of coherent overall system, but we would be missing the thrust of his work, which upsets all these categories and their neat systematicity. Indeed, one may well suggest that there is too much 'logic' involved in such parcelling out of subjects, or the wrong sort of logic, namely one that turns theology into an object. One *should not* build a metaphysical system of theology from Marion's work because it refuses such a system at its very core, instead calling us to do theology in a very different mode: as the response to a call, as the unfolding of God's self-manifestation, as the dis-covery of God's invisibility in the face of Christ, explicating what it means to say that 'God was in Christ reconciling all the world to himself' (2 Cor. 5.19). The various 'topics' of theology are then intricately connected; it is not possible to speak of salvation apart from speaking of Christ or to speak of the human apart from the divine. Theology is concerned with the unfolding of God's revelation as it is manifested in our lives and in the life of the church. It is, then, a theology of experience, of our experience of the divine in the crossing of gazes in prayer and in love, if we are willing to expose ourselves to it and bear its impact.

A theology that tries to be a science or that assumes a metaphysical system misses its very task and is doomed to idolatry.

In evaluating the 'theological status' of St Augustine's work, Marion repeatedly refers somewhat dismissively to a definition of 'theology' as 'a speculative discourse *about* God, as modern usage would have it' (SP, 11). Augustine does not speak about God but to God. To think of theology primarily as speech about God has serious consequences:

> To speak *of* God would mean in the end speaking *of* him but *without*, indeed *against*, him. Philosophy does not prohibit itself from doing so, nor, for the most part, does theology. In opposition, speaking *to* God, as the confessing praise does, implies first of all turning one's face *to* God so that he can come over me, claim me, and call me starting from himself, well beyond what I could say, predict, or predicate of him starting from myself alone. (SP, 19)

Theology, then, is preceded by God's naming in Scripture and always an unfolding of the word as it is already spoken before me and to me. Theology must arise out of confession, but that confession is also already a citation of the words that have preceded me. Not even confession is 'authentic' in the sense of autonomous and autarchic. Authentic theology is 'inauthentic' inasmuch as it is not one's own, but the unfolding of revelation within the biblical and patristic tradition. It is in this sense that the *Confessions* might be read as 'an immense treatise of speculative theology' (SP, 291), namely as a reflection on how to name God in prayerful praise.

On a few occasions Marion addresses the topic of theology head-on. In *God without Being*, which at least within the text (though sometimes not in retrospect) he identifies as an essay in theology, he speaks of the pleasure and the terror of writing theology (GWB, 1). Theology must speak of God from the point of view of the Word, which means 'that this theology should expose its logic to the repercussions, within it, of the *theos*' (GWB, 139). Above all, theology speaks of Christ who himself points to God and is the Word of God. Christ's word must become flesh in us: 'To justify its Christianity, a theology must be conceived as a *logos* of the *Logos*, a word of the Word, a said of the Said' (GWB, 143). This means that we must ultimately speak from God's point of view: 'The theologian must go beyond the text to the Word, interpreting it from the point of view of the Word' (GWB, 149).

But it does not mean that we speak from some sort of privileged position, rather that we allow God to speak through us: 'To do theology is not to speak the language of gods or of "God," but to let the Word speak us' (GWB, 143). *Theo*-logy must be informed by a eucharistic hermeneutic that speaks from the standpoint of the cross. And this is not an individual activity but rather a communal or ecclesial one: 'The community therefore interprets the text in view of its referent only to the strict degree that it lets itself be called together and assimilated, hence converted and interpreted by the Word, sacramentally and therefore actually acting in the community' (GWB, 152). We interpret together as a community as we live the reality of the faith sacramentally.

While Marion is often thought – not incorrectly – to advocate an apophatic theology that stresses God's transcendence, in a different sense his theology can be said to be one of radical immanence, of complete and utter self-revelation of the divine. It is right that he stresses God's incomprehensible and unconditioned character, that he forbids all metaphysical talk about God as idolatrous, that he rejects proofs for God's existence and even speaks of God 'without Being'. And yet, in some ways that opens the path for an equally radical focus on God's utter immanence, disclosure, manifestation, revelation. Marion's phenomenology can in some sense be said to be dedicated to describing carefully how God is given, manifested and revealed, namely in love and gift. Phenomenology cannot examine God's transcendence and alterity and it rightly guards against making claims about them. But, in Marion's view, it can and should devote itself to unfolding God's immanence, the divine self-revelation in Christ.

It is possible, then, that Marion's thought may challenge us to overcome some of the divisions we tend to draw in theology, separating 'systematic' from 'practical' theology, 'biblical' from 'liturgical' (and certainly again from 'systematic') theology, or dividing it into periods: patristic, medieval, modern, contemporary theology – as if the time period were somehow more important than the content. One cannot speak *of* God (except idolatrously or metaphysically) without speaking *to* God: theology is address. This address is at the same time an attempt to approach the divine. Knowing God means not to speculate about God but to experience God and to seek to articulate that experience as fully and faithfully as possible. This does not mean, obviously, that theology becomes merely an existential venting about one's personal experience of God. Marion's work is not only itself rigorous and often difficult, but he argues throughout for the rationality of faith and theology. Yet, this rationality is an unfolding of the logos, of God's reason as it is revealed in Christ, rather than the imposition of a foreign (metaphysical) rationality. That does not mean that theology must become incoherent or without reason. Rather, for Marion, theology flows from the logic of the cross, from an alternative rationality that challenges our preconceptions. Marion's work calls us to dispense with metaphysical construction and instead to think theologically in the mode of revelation, that is to say, in a phenomenological mode. It does not allow for any separation between 'theoretical' and 'practical' theology, but instead theology is the unfolding of liturgical practice and the experience of God.

God is experienced most fully and most authentically in prayer and worship, in the lives of those who are baptized into the name of God through Christ in the Spirit. This may also call us to get beyond our curiously modern obsession with considering doctrinal questions in isolation, which often leads us to regard only those patristic texts of importance that wrangle over christological or trinitarian questions, while ignoring homiletic or liturgical material. Why should, for instance, Gregory of Nyssa's arguments against Eunomius over the 'unbegottenness' of the Son be judged so much more weighty theologically than, for example, Gregory Nazianzen's poetry or his beautiful homily on 'New Sunday', which I would hazard to guess was read far more frequently in church over the centuries than the treatises against the Arians and affected the life of the church more deeply.

Although Marion does not cite it, what he says is certainly congruent with Evagrius of Pontus' famous statement that 'if you are a theologian you will pray truly and if you pray truly you are a theologian'. Theology is unfolded from prayer, from the exposure to the gaze that meets me across the icon, from the gift I receive in the Eucharist, from the liturgical life of the church. Theology that is not grounded in prayer, in these experiences of God's manifestation, is idle speculation, or worse, blasphemous idolatry. If theology does not guide us to Christ, does not open us to God's gift, does not teach us to love, it is not theology but only mental experimentation: 'The theological teacher is not justified unless he serves charity. Otherwise, he brings death. But, the more the teacher inscribes himself in the eucharistic rite opened by the bishop, the more he can become a *theo*logian' (GWB, 154). Theology does not speak itself, but allows another to speak within it. Thus, theology is always on some level hypocritical, because it can really only be done by the saints, by those who might be able to speak of God authentically because the unseen God is manifested in them. It requires holiness and transformation of life: 'theology cannot aim at any other progress than its own conversion to the Word' (GWB, 158). Theology must unfold the gift given in incarnation, manifestation, revelation.

All this suggests, finally, that 'spirituality' and 'liturgy' are not separate subjects from theology, but if theology is prayer then it is also liturgy and spirituality: an account of God's self-manifestation in the life of the Christian, in the life of the church. Theology, then, might be more about explicating the rigour of its own liturgical practice, rather than an abstract mental or purely academic exercise removed from the prayerful life of the church and the believer. This is why it is so deeply sacramental, so strongly focused on the Eucharist – the manifestation of Christ's body as it is broken and given to us as a gift of love, and we become incorporated into it as body of Christ, as people of God, as the ones bearing Christ's invisible face and making it present in the world. That requires, as it did for Christ, kenotic self-abandon, unconditional love, pouring oneself out as gift for the other to the point of death. And it requires praise, prayer, hence liturgy. This suggests that, as many liturgical theologians now claim, liturgical theology is 'primary theology' and that theology cannot be abstracted from the ascetical, spiritual and liturgical life of the church – or becomes abstracted from it only to its own detriment. Indeed, in his book on Augustine, Marion says: 'This question asks about the *liturgical and therefore theological* conditions for the praise of God and considers creation only as an output of the hermeneutic operation of praise – in and through the interpretation of heaven and earth *as* created and *as* silently proclaiming not themselves but God' (SP, 237; first emphasis mine). Here the liturgical and the theological are explicitly equated with each other.

As already cited in the introduction, Marion suggests that the practice of prayer and the experience of the sacrament means that 'one can no longer place speculative theology or neutral rationality to one side and the spiritual life to the other, but the same place encompasses both' (RC, 53). We can now see how that is true of Marion's work as a whole. This unification of 'rationality' and 'spirituality' is what he shows about Descartes, whose defence of the creation of the eternal truths and arguments against univocal namings of God are as much about standing veiled before God in prayer as they are about philosophical speculation. They come together in the third order of charity, which is not only an alternative form of knowing but also its loving embrace. They come together when we approach God via the icon, where we also expose ourselves to the divine gaze. They come together when we experience the phenomenon of revelation as it is given to us abundantly and, at the same time, postulates the parameters according to which it gives itself on its own terms. They come together when we receive this phenomenon as the gift of love, when we allow ourselves to become converted in a counter-experience in which we are no longer the controlling subject but the devoted recipient. And they especially come together and reach their height in the rationality of faith and the practices of prayer and sacramental participation that effect the conversion of the baptized. Thus, the unfolding of revelation as the manifestation of God's givenness in Christ through the Spirit to the church is the 'speculative knowledge' – or rather, alternative 'rationality' appropriate to revealed theology – that spiritually folds us into the life of God through Christ in the Spirit. Ultimately theology is to lead us into the divine life: 'Thus, confessio alone unites with God, not mere knowledge, which remains only a means and a mode of it' (SP, 248). Marion's theology, if it can be called that, is a theology of response and receptivity, a theology that works out the phenomenon of revelation that has been given to us by the theological and liturgical labour of learning to live it in love. Theology does not impose parameters upon God but tries to unfold the claim made upon us, the given of experience, most supremely the abundant givenness of the eucharistic gift of the broken body and shed blood. Theology, then, is spirituality: prayer, praise, participation.

BIBLIOGRAPHY

Selected Works in English by Marion

(listed by the order of their original publication in French)

The Idol and Distance: Five Studies (trans. Thomas A. Carlson; New York: Fordham University Press, 2001).

God without Being (trans. Thomas A. Carlson; Chicago: University of Chicago Press, 1991; 2nd edn, 2012).

Prolegomena to Charity (trans. Stephen E. Lewis; New York: Fordham University Press, 2002).

On Descartes' Metaphysical Prism: The Constitution and the Limits of Onto-theo-logy in Cartesian Thought (trans. Jeffrey L. Kosky; Chicago: University of Chicago Press, 1999).

Reduction and Givenness: Investigations of Husserl, Heidegger, and Phenomenology (trans. Thomas A. Carlson; Evanston: Northwestern University Press, 1998).

The Crossing of the Visible (trans. James K. A. Smith; Stanford, CA: Stanford University Press, 2004).

Cartesian Questions: Method and Metaphysics (Chicago: University of Chicago Press, 1999).

'Saint Thomas Aquinas and Onto-theo-logy' in *Mystic: Presence and Aporia* (ed. M. Kessler and C. Sheppard; Chicago: University of Chicago Press, 2003), 38–74.

On the Ego and on God: Further Cartesian Questions (trans. Christina M. Gschwandtner; New York: Fordham University Press, 2007).

Being Given: Toward a Phenomenology of Givenness (trans. Jeffrey L. Kosky; Stanford, CA: Stanford University Press, 2002).

In Excess: Studies of Saturated Phenomena (trans. Robyn Horner and Vincent Berraud; New York: Fordham University Press, 2002).

The Erotic Phenomenon (trans. Stephen E. Lewis; Chicago: University of Chicago Press, 2003).

The Visible and the Revealed (New York: Fordham University Press, 2008).

In the Self's Place: The Approach of Saint Augustine (trans. Jeffrey L. Kosky; Stanford, CA: Stanford University Press, 2012).

Negative Certainties (trans. Stephen E. Lewis; Chicago: University of Chicago Press, 2015).

Believing in Order to See (trans. Christina M. Gschwandtner; New York: Fordham University Press, 2016).

The Reason of the Gift (ed. and trans. Stephen E. Lewis; Charlottesville: University of Virginia Press, 2011).

'What We See and What Appears', in *Idol Anxiety* (ed. Josh Ellenbogen and Aaron Tugendhaft; Stanford: Stanford University Press, 2011), 152–68.

The Rigor of Things. Conversations with Dan Arbib (trans. Christina M. Gschwandtner; New York: Fordham University Press, 2016).

Givenness and Hermeneutics (The Père Marquette Lecture in Theology 2013; trans. Jean-Pierre Lafouge; Milwaukee: Marquette University Press, 2012).

'The Question of the Unconditioned', *Journal of Religion* 93 (1) (2013): 1–24.

The Essential Writings (ed. Kevin Hart; New York: Fordham University Press, 2013).

Givenness and Revelation (trans. Stephen E. Lewis; Oxford: Oxford University Press, 2016).

Selected Works in English about Marion

Benson, Bruce Ellis, *Graven Ideologies: Nietzsche, Derrida and Marion on Modern Idolatry* (Downers Grove, IL: InterVarsity Press, 2002).

Burch, Matthew I., 'Blurred Vision: Marion on the "Possibility" of Revelation', *International Journal for Philosophy of Religion* 67 (3) (2010): 157–71.

Caputo, John D., 'God Is Wholly Other – Almost: "Difference" and the Hyperbolic Alterity of God', in *The Otherness of God* (ed. Orrin F. Summerell; Charlottesville: University Press of Virginia, 1998), 190–205.

Caputo, John D., 'Apostles of the Impossible: On God and the Gift in Derrida and Marion', in *God, the Gift, and Postmodernism* (ed. John D. Caputo and Michael J. Scanlon; Bloomington: Indiana University Press, 1999), 185–222.

Caputo, John D., 'The Poetics of the Impossible and the Kingdom of God', in *Rethinking Philosophy of Religion: Approaches from*

Continental Philosophy (ed. Philip Goodchild; New York: Fordham University Press, 2002), 42–58.

Carlson, Thomas A., *Indiscretion: Finitude and the Naming of God* (Chicago: University of Chicago Press, 1999).

Cooke, Alexander, 'What Saturates? Jean-Luc Marion's Phenomenological Theology', *Philosophy Today* 48 (2) (2004): 179–87.

Dodd, James, 'Marion and Phenomenology', *Graduate Faculty Philosophy Journal* 25 (1) (2004): 161–84.

Faulconer, James E. (ed.), *Transcendence in Philosophy and Religion* (Bloomington: Indiana University Press, 2003).

Gschwandtner, Christina M., *Reading Jean-Luc Marion: Exceeding Metaphysics* (Bloomington: Indiana University Press, 2007).

Gschwandtner, Christina M., *Degrees of Givenness: On Saturation in Jean-Luc Marion* (Bloomington: Indiana University Press, 2014).

Hanson, Jeffrey A., 'Jean-Luc Marion and the Possibility of a Post-Modern Theology', *Mars Hill Review* 12 (1998): 93–104.

Hart, Kevin (ed.), *Counter-Experiences: Reading Jean-Luc Marion* (South Bend, IN: Notre Dame University Press, 2007).

Horner, Robyn, *Rethinking God as Gift: Derrida, Marion, and the Limits of Phenomenology* (New York: Fordham University Press, 2001).

Horner, Robyn, *Jean-Luc Marion: A Theo-logical Introduction* (Hants: Ashgate, 2005).

Janicaud, Dominique, Jean-François Courtine, Jean-Louis Chrétien, Michel Henry, Jean-Luc Marion and Paul Ricœur, *Phenomenology and the "Theological Turn": The French Debate* (New York: Fordham University Press, 2000).

Janicaud, Dominique, *Phenomenology "Wide Open": After the French Debate* (trans. Charles N. Cabral; New York: Fordham University Press, 2005).

Jones, Tamsin, *A Genealogy of Marion's Philosophy of Religion: Apparent Darkness* (Bloomington: Indiana University Press, 2011).

Kosky, Jeffrey L., 'Philosophy of Religion and Return to Phenomenology in Jean-Luc Marion: From *God without Being* to *Being Given*', *American Catholic Philosophical Quarterly* 78 (4) (2004): 629–47.

Leask, Ian and Eoin Cassidy (eds), *Givenness and God: Questions of Jean-Luc Marion* (New York: Fordham University Press, 2005).

Mackinlay, Shane, 'Eyes Wide Shut: A Response to Jean-Luc Marion's Account of the Journey to Emmaus', *Modern Theology* 20 (3) (2004): 447–56.

Mackinlay, Shane, *Interpreting Excess: Jean-Luc Marion, Saturated Phenomena, and Hermeneutics* (New York: Fordham University Press, 2010).

Manolopoulos, Mark, *If Creation Is a Gift* (Albany: State University of New York Press, 2009).

Manoussakis, John P., *God After Metaphysics: A Theological Aesthetic* (Bloomington: Indiana University Press, 2007).

Miller, Adam S., *Badiou, Marion and St. Paul: Immanent Grace* (London: Continuum, 2008).

Morrow, Derek J., 'Aquinas According to the Horizon of Distance: Jean-Luc Marion's Phenomenological reading of Thomistic Analogy', *International Philosophical Quarterly* 47 (1) (2007): 59–77.

Morrow, Derek J., 'The Love "without Being" That Opens (To) Distance, Part One: Exploring the Givenness of the Erotic Phenomenon with Jean-Luc Marion', *Heythrop Journal: A Bimonthly Review of Philosophy and Theology* 46 (3) (2005): 281–98.

Morrow, Derek J., 'The Love "without Being" That Opens (To) Distance, Part Two: From the Icon of Distance to the Distance of the Icon in Marion's Phenomenology of Love', *Heythrop Journal: A Bimonthly Review of Philosophy and Theology* 46 (4) (2005): 493–511.

Rottenberg, Ian, 'Fine Art as a Preparation for Christian Love', *Journal of Religious Ethics* 42 (2) (2014): 243–62.

Schrijvers, Joeri, 'In (the) Place of the Self: A Critical Study of Jean-Luc Marion's *Au Lieu de soi. L'approche de Saint Augustin*', *Modern Theology* 25 (4) (2009): 661–86.

Schrijvers, Joeri, 'Jean-Luc Marion and the Transcendence "par Excellence": Love', in *Looking Beyond? Shifting Views of Transcendence in Philosophy, Theology, Art, and Politics* (ed. Wessel Stoker and W. L. van der Merwe; New York and Amsterdam: Rodopi, 2011).

Schrijvers, Joeri, *Ontotheological Turnings? The Decentering of the Modern Subject in Recent French Phenomenology* (Albany: State University of New York Press, 2011).

Smit, Peter-Ben, 'The Bishop and His/Her Eucharistic Community: A Critique of Jean-Luc Marion's Eucharistic Hermeneutic', *Modern Theology* 19 (1) (2003): 29–40.

Steinbock, Anthony, 'The Poor Phenomenon: Marion and the Problem of Givenness', in *Words of Life: New Theological Turns in French Phenomenology* (ed. Bruce Ellis Benson and Norman Wirzba; New York: Fordham University Press, 2010), 120–31.

Tóth, Beáta, 'Love between Embodiment and Spirituality: Jean-Luc Marion and John Paul II on Erotic Love', *Modern Theology* 29 (1) (2013): 18–47.

Wallenfang, Donald L., 'Sacramental Givenness: The Notion of Givenness in Husserl, Heidegger, and Marion, and Its Import for

Interpreting the Phenomenality of the Eucharist', *Philosophy and Theology: Marquette University Quarterly* 22 (1–2) (2010): 131–54.

Ward, Graham, 'The Theological Project of Jean-Luc Marion', in *Post-secular Philosophy: Between Philosophy and Theology* (ed. Phillip Blond; New York and London: Routledge, 1998).

Wardley, Kenneth Jason, '"A Desire unto Death": The Deconstructive Thanatology of Jean-Luc Marion', *Heythrop Journal: A Bimonthly Review of Philosophy and Theology* 49 (1) (2008): 79–96.

Welten, Ruud, 'The Paradox of God's Appearance: On Jean-Luc Marion', in *God in France: Eight Contemporary French Thinkers on God* (ed. Peter Jonkers and Ruud Welten; Leuven, Belgium: Peeters, 2005), 186–206.

Westphal, Merold, 'Transfiguration as Saturated Phenomenon', *Philosophy and Scripture* 1 (1) (2003): 1–10.

Westphal, Merold, 'Vision and Voice: Phenomenology and Theology in the Work of Jean-Luc Marion', *International Journal for Philosophy of Religion* 60 (1–3) (2006): 117–37.

INDEX